Sallie Elizabeth Joy White

**Cookery in the Public Schools**

Sallie Elizabeth Joy White

**Cookery in the Public Schools**

ISBN/EAN: 9783744788199

Printed in Europe, USA, Canada, Australia, Japan

Cover: Foto ©Andreas Hilbeck / pixelio.de

More available books at **www.hansebooks.com**

# COOKERY IN
# THE PUBLIC SCHOOLS

BY

SALLIE JOY WHITE

Author of "House Keepers and Home Makers."

*Illustrated*

BOSTON
D LOTHROP COMPANY
WASHINGTON STREET OPPOSITE BROMFIELD

COPYRIGHT, 1890,
BY
D. LOTHROP COMPANY.

# PREFACE.

IN sending out this little book, the result of a careful watchfulness of the public school kitchen work, from its inception to the present time, the hope has been to interest communities beyond Boston in the idea of industrial training in the public schools, and to give the girls themselves some idea of the value of the teaching. Only a hint has been given of the real amount of work, but I hope it is sufficient to make all who read feel the need of increasing it. I am deeply indebted to Miss Homans, who has given me access to the schools, allowed me the use of the rules, and the privilege of copying the charts and tables. If the work of establishing cookery as a branch of training in the schools generally is permanently successful, it will be because of the devoted work of this noble woman, who has carried to the finest and fullest completion the plans of Mrs. Mary Hemenway, who supported the first school kitchen, and now supports the Normal Training School for preparing teachers in cooking for the public schools.

SALLIE JOY WHITE.

ASHCROFT, Dedham,
 *March* 15, 1890.

TO
*AMY MORRIS HOMANS,*
WITH THE GRATITUDE AND REGARD OF
THE AUTHOR.

# CONTENTS.

### CHAPTER I.

MASTER ALLEN'S PROPHECY . . . 7

### CHAPTER II.

FIRE-BUILDING . . . . . . . 22

### CHAPTER III.

SOME SIMPLE USES OF THE OVEN . . . 40

### CHAPTER IV.

A LESSON IN BOILING. . . . . . 53

### CHAPTER V.

GOING TO MARKET . . . . 69

### CHAPTER VI.

MEATS AND MADE-OVERS . . . . . 83

### CHAPTER VII.

SOUPS AND STEWS . . . . . . 98

## CHAPTER VIII.

A LESSON IN BATTERS . . . . . 114

## CHAPTER IX.

BREAD-MAKING . . . . . . 128

## CHAPTER X.

FISH AND EGG DISHES . . . 139

## CHAPTER XI.

INVALID COOKERY . . . . . . 149

## CHAPTER XII.

NORMAL TRAINING . . . . . . · 164

# COOKERY
# IN THE PUBLIC SCHOOLS

## CHAPTER I.

MASTER ALLEN'S PROPHECY.

TWENTY-FIVE years ago, Master Allen, the head of the Hancock School in Boston, said contemptuously: "Teach sewing in the public schools! The next thing we know they will be for setting up cook-stoves in our schoolrooms, and asking us to teach the girls to make bread and broil beefsteak!"

To Master Allen's mind, that was the very height of impossibility; the very remotest contingency; and in making the remark he felt that he was giving full expression to the fine scorn with which he regarded the innovation of needle and thimble.

And yet, what he considered as impossible has come about. What do you suppose Master Allen would say could he take a peep now, during any school day, into the finely-appointed kitchen in the basement of the Tennyson Street Schoolhouse in Boston, and see the interested girls in white caps and aprons, learning how to become good housekeepers and cooks? He would be utterly bewildered with it all; and unless he has grown much wiser in his new environment, he would think, no doubt, that a backward step had been taken in the modes of education.

But people have had time and opportunity to learn many things since the stubborn principal of the large North End School held such despotic sway; and among the things that have been learned is a lesson that it has taken much time to impress upon the minds of those who have had the public schools and their management in charge.

It was this: that the education being given to the children was a very one-sided one, and that while it gave a great deal of information that might, or might not, be of value to those who obtained it, there was a decided lack of practical instruction, so that when the boys and girls left the schools, they had absolutely no working capital.

The few people who first felt this truth, and dared to speak about it, and to suggest that there should be some change in the plan of instruction, were laughed at as "silly folk" who must find fault with something. The word "crank" had not then taken its place in the current vocabulary; but you know nowadays it is shouted derisively after every one who dares to advance an opinion that differs from the one held by the majority. That is what the early advocates of industrial education would have been called had the word then existed with its present significance.

But all the scorn that was heaped upon the advocates of the new education, and all the ridicule, could not make them believe themselves anything but right; and by degrees they drew other people to their own way of thinking, until, before the great public knew anything about it, there was a large number of persons, including the wisest men and women of the time, protesting against this one-sided instruction that trained the head at the expense of the hands. What these far-sighted people believed in, was a school-system that would provide an "all round" education.

The first result of the agitation was the introduction of sewing into the public schools, as a two-hours exercise each week. There were a great many protestants against the innovation beside Master Allen; but the reason his protest is specially remembered is on account of the prophecy which it contained. No doubt he would have been as unwilling a prophet as he was an unconscious one, but a prophet he was, notwithstanding.

Well, the sewing was introduced, and it did not overturn the schools, nor demoralize the pupils. But the sharp little needles, in the hands of the willing girls, went on pricking individual prejudices, until by and by the very people who had opposed it, were its warm friends and advocates. The teachers said that the children worked better at their books for the change of employment; that the heads rested while the hands worked, and that a deal of dangerous nervous restlessness was carried off through the stitches. Mothers were proud of the work their girls could do, and the girls themselves grew particular about the appearance of their clothing, taking better care of it since they knew the labor of making, and had acquired the knack of repairing.

It is no wonder when the experiment of sewing was found to be a success, that the people who had been instrumental in bringing it about, should look around for another department of industry to introduce. But it is a wonder that it was going to be as necessary to convert the public to the new work, as it had been to the sewing.

But a wise woman who has proven her wisdom in many ways in forwarding education, and helping boys and girls to become useful men and women, decided that it was better to prove the usefulness of the measure first, then, should it be necessary, to argue about it afterwards. Mrs. Mary Hemenway, who had supported the Old South Free Lectures for the children of the Boston schools, who had founded schools for the poor children in the South, who had offered and bestowed the prizes for the essays in American History to be written by the graduates of the High Schools, had also for a number of years supported a summer school in the Tennyson Street Schoolhouse, where girls have been taught several branches of industry, including even light carpentering and cabinet-making. After watching her experiments for several seasons, Mrs. Hemenway decided that the best industry to introduce into the public schools would be cooking. She did not talk much about her plan; she asked the School Committee to let her keep the kitchen she had so beautifully fitted up, and to allow classes of girls from several of the schools to be sent during the year for instruction in cooking, which she would provide at her own expense.

It may be that the School Committee were rather anxious to have such an experiment tried. At any event, they gave Mrs. Hemenway ready permission to keep the kitchen, and heartily accepted the very generous proposition that she made them.

So the school was begun. There were two classes, of fifteen girls each, that met every day to learn the mysteries of cooking. Each girl who came to the school took only one half a day each week from her book-studies; and no girl was allowed to attend whose mother did not fully approve of her doing so.

The pupils were marked for tardiness or for absence, exactly as they were at the school itself; for the cooking, like the sewing, was considered a part of the school-training, and a regular school-exercise, at which the girls were still held under the rules.

At first the pupils themselves did not quite know whether to like the new departure or not. It was something so new, so utterly out of the every-day school routine. But as most girls have the natural instinct of the housewife, that waits only occasion to arouse, they soon found that the new duty was very pleasant.

In the first place, they had such a perfectly appointed kitchen to work in! It was a real delight to be in it, and to be allowed to handle all the convenient implements at will, with the feeling of absolute proprietorship. There were closets and cupboards filled with stores, and with pretty dishes; a large range, always kept bright and shining, and that looked cheerful from very cleanliness, even when there was no fire in it; an abundance of towels and dishcloths, and, best of all, a large circular table, divided into compartments, each one having its own gas stove, its spoons, its mixing dishes and measuring cups, its bread-board and rolling-pin, its egg-beaters and strainers — all the conveniences, indeed, that could be needed for personal use in cooking. Each girl had her cap and apron, usually a long tier with sleeves, that covered her from the throat of her dress to the hem, protecting it from all traces of the work in which she was engaged. With her apron and cap, her holder and towel pinned to her side, she was ready to begin her work, and, as a general thing, every one of the pupils felt a real enthusiasm after the first strangeness was over.

For three years Mrs. Hemenway continued her experiment; now the city has taken the school, and established others as well in different parts of the city, so that during the year eighteen hundred and eighty-eight eighteen hundred girls received good training in cooking. There has been no need for argument; the experiment has been proof, as Mrs. Hemenway was sure it would be; everybody is praising the cooking as they have before praised the sewing.

But the best of it all is to hear the mothers talk about it; they are so delighted with the results that they have nothing but thankfulness toward the system. You see the girls do not merely learn their lessons in theory, but they really do the work themselves, and then go home and cook the same dishes for the family meals, so that the mothers and fathers have an opportunity of testing for themselves the value of the teaching. And they are very proud when they can treat some visitor to a specially nice dish and say, —

"It was made by daughter; she learned it at school."

A mother said to me while telling about some trouble she had had with a servant, which resulted in her sending the girl away:

"Annie"—that was her daughter who had graduated from the grammar school a little less than a year before—"says I shall not be bothered with another servant; she is going to do the family cooking. And oh! it is such a comfort and rest to have her do it. She is so economical, and so nice about it, and she really enjoys it herself so much! I would much rather she did this than went out of her home to work, as she would. So I have told her that I would pay her just what I had been paying a girl. She will have her own income, and we will have good cooking and nice housekeeping. I feel the relief already."

Wasn't that a jolly, comfortable way of fixing things? And wouldn't many a girl like it, if she could be the mother's helper in such a fashion? And that is just what the cooking-schools are making possible, both for mothers and daughters; and, between you and me, I think it is going some way in solving the perplexing question of domestic service and inefficient help, that we all hear so much about in these days. There is a chance for a good long look ahead in this subject, and one day you and I will look back over the ground that has been trodden, and wonder that the public teaching of cookery wasn't thought about earlier.

In the schools now, whenever there is a sewing exhibition, there is a cooking exhibition as well; and after the visitors have admired the nicely made under-clothing, bed and table linen, and wondered at the skill and proficiency which made it possible for such young needlewomen to compass the dresses, complete infants' wardrobes, and boys' suits, that are spread out for them to see, each with the name and age of the youthful seamstress pinned to it, they are asked to another room. And there they are shown fine loaves of bread, nicely cooked meats, fish and vegetables, gruels and beef tea, jellies and blanc-manges, that are also labelled with the name and age of the makers. You will not find many loaves of cake, or pies, or much "fancy cooking," for the school teaches the common-sense of cookery; believing if the pupils learn the principles thoroughly they can do very much themselves with practice.

Now as there are so many young people who have not the opportunity of learning what is taught the fortunate girls in the Boston schools, I propose telling you a little bit of what these same girls really learn, trusting that it may interest you so much that you will all become earnest advocates of a system of education that shall embrace some of the industries, and shall place value on the work of the hands as well as of the head.

Because you are not where you have the advantage of the training of these schools, you need not think it is of no use for you to want it. By no means. Other cities and towns are following the example of Boston, and are introducing the teaching of cooking into their public schools; and if you are really in earnest in your desire, you may impart your interest to others, and out of the growth of this interest may come the very thing you want. Public-spirited girls have a chance to make a great many advance steps in any good movement. There is no telling what they may bring about by talking with their parents over the morning coffee.

There are teachers in training now to take positions in schools as teachers of cookery, and those already graduated have found places in New England cities, and in the South and West. One young colored woman came from the Tuskagee College in Alabama to prepare herself to take the department of cooking in that institution, and she has finished her course and gone to her work full of enthusiasm for it.

In most of the cities the school is supported from the school-fund, a special appropriation being made for it; in other places it is carried on by private generosity. Mr. Augustus Hemenway, the son of Mrs. Hemenway who began the work in Boston, has followed his mother's example and has established a school in Canton, Mass., the town in which he lives, and still another in Easton, Mass.

# CHAPTER II.

### FIRE-BUILDING.

THE roll is called, the girls are in their uniforms — that is, the apron, the cap, the holder suspended by a tape from the belt, always in readiness for use, and the hand-towel pinned to the side. Rings and bracelets — if any one is so thoughtless as to wear them to a cooking-lesson — are laid aside, the hands are washed, and the nails looked after; for an important feature of the first lesson, as well as of every succeeding one, is that of personal cleanliness. And it is repeated all the way along too. The hands are washed as often as needed; and always before touching any food they are wiped on the towel at the side. That is why the towel hangs there.

The three housekeepers are chosen; out of each class of fifteen, three are called housekeepers, while the rest are cooks. The three housekeepers do the kitchen work, and each one has her own special set of duties.

The lists of duties for the housekeepers are printed plainly on a blackboard, so that each knows just what she has to do, and there is no interference of tasks between the three. In this way everything is done at its own proper time, and by the proper person. The rules for the housekeepers are like this:*

### HOUSEKEEPER NUMBER ONE.

Get kindlings and coal.
Build the fire.
Regulate the dampers.
Empty ashes into sifter.
Brush the stove under and around it.
Blacken the stove.
Light the fire.
Polish the stove.
Regulate the dampers.

---

* These rules are copied from the blackboard of School Kitchen No. 1, where they were placed in October, 1886.

Fill tea-kettle and reservoir with fresh water.
Wash the hearth or zinc under the stove.
Wash the cloth and put to dry.
Sift the ashes.
Bring the cinders to the kitchen.

This is what Housekeeper Number One has to do in the morning class. The Afternoon Housekeeper Number One must

Regulate the fire.
Replenish the kettles.
Empty the kettles and copper boiler, and turn them over to dry.

The last things, of course, are to be done when the lesson is ended.

### HOUSEKEEPER NUMBER TWO.

Dust the room thoroughly. Begin at one corner, and take each article in turn. Dust from the highest things to the lowest, taking up the dust in the cloth, but not brushing it off on the floor. Shake the duster occasionally in a suitable place, and when through, wash and hang it to dry.

Bring the stores to teacher when directed.

Scrub the dresser and teacher's desk.

A SCHOOL KITCHEN.

*(Showing compartments around table with gas stoves, etc.)*

Keep the dresser in perfect order.
Wipe dishes if needed.
Sweep the room when the lesson is over, beginning at one side, and sweeping toward one place. Hold the broom close to the floor; sweep with short strokes, and let the broom take the dust along the floor, instead of tossing it into the air.

## HOUSEKEEPER NUMBER THREE.

Polish the boiler.
Clean knives and spoons in dresser drawer.
Wash and wipe dishes.
Wash dish towels.
Scrub sink outside and in with hot suds.
Wash cloth and hang to dry.

I think it wouldn't be a half-bad idea to have a set of similar rules, condensed for family purposes, printed and hung in every kitchen; though I'm not at all sure that you could get the girls to read them. The home-girls would, but the hired ones wouldn't.

Of course the same girls do not act as housekeepers all the time. It is arranged that these duties are shared in alternation, in order that every pupil may learn both the cooking and the kitchen work.

When everything is in readiness the teacher gives the pupils a little preliminary talk about cooking in general, and they bring out their note-books and pencils, and write down all the points she gives them, so that they may be ready to answer the questions at the next lesson. And more than this, they must remember it, for they have to be examined in their knowledge of this branch of study as in any other, and are marked by the same system of percentage.

In the first place the teacher gives them the definition of cooking; and they are told that it is the preparation of food by the aid of heat to nourish the human body: Food is cooked to render it more palatable, and more easy of digestion; to make it assimilate with our bodies, and do us good by giving us strength. Among the agents necessary for cooking, the most important are heat, liquid and air. Then follows a short lesson on practical chemistry, giving special information about the four most important elements, namely, oxygen, nitrogen, hydrogen and carbon.

Then follows the lesson on fire-building, the teacher superintending and giving the directions, and Housekeeper Number One following them, while the rest of the class look on and listen. It is only in the early lessons that the instruction is needed; after a while the girls get to be the most expert fire-builders that can be imagined, and what is quite as much to the purpose, as every housekeeper of experience will tell you, they know how to tend it and keep it with economy; something, by the way, that a good many housekeepers themselves do not understand. You see the mere "knowing how" to do anything, isn't all there is of a lesson. You must understand how to make the knowledge attained available; that is the true education. A person may acquire a knowledge of a great many things, but if she doesn't know what use to make of it she might as well be without it, for all the real good it does her. She is not educated; she is merely hampered with a lot of useless facts that lumber her intellect with cumbersome stuff.

But we are learning to make a fire; and the first thing to be done is to remove all the covers from the stove, and brush all the ashes from the top of the inside into the fire-box; this keeps the heat channel clear, and makes the oven easier to heat, and keeps the stove in constant cleanliness. Then the covers are replaced and the dampers closed. This, you will understand, is done to keep the fine dust from escaping when you empty the contents of the fire-box into the pan. Most kitchen girls neglect this precaution, and then wonder why they have so much dust in their kitchens. The Boston public school-girls could tell them all about it. When the stove has been closed as tightly as possible, the directions are to turn over the grate, letting the contents fall into the ash-pan below. Turn the grate back to its place, after clearing it of any clinging substance. Brush out the oven after the dust has ceased to rise, and then it will be clean for use and free from dust when you are ready to bake in it. If there should not be a double grate, as there is not except in some of the newest ranges, remove the ashes and cinders together and sift them. Always take out the ashes before lighting the fire, for if they are left in the pan, sparks and lighted coals will drop into them. It is then very unsafe to remove them unless you have a fire-proof ash-receiver. Fires are often traceable to the careless disposition of hot ashes. You can readily see what mischief might occur from putting ashes containing live coals into a wooden barrel or box.

And now that the stove is cleaned and the ashes and cinders taken care of the next thing is to make the fire. Of course you all know without telling that the fire box is the part of the stove or range that holds the fire. Now into this fire box you want to put, first of all, loose pieces of newspaper, that have been torn in strips; these go at the very bottom, resting on the grate; use plenty of paper, so that the kindling may have a chance to light before the paper is burned out. Next, lay small pieces of light wood across the box, leaving little spaces between the pieces; on these put a layer of kindling a little larger than the first layer, putting the sticks at right angles with the lower ones; on these again place fine hard wood kindling, then larger hard wood, and finally a thin layer of small coal. In this way you will have little trouble in making the fire burn. Each layer, as it burns, heats the one above it. Now you see there is a distinction between building a fire and lighting it.

Now the fire is built, and the covers are replaced. The housekeeper starts to light the fire, but on being referred to her rules, she finds that the next thing to be done is to open the dampers, remove the ash-pan and sift the ashes,

BUILDING A FIRE.

replace the pan, and brush the dust off the stove. Then she blackens her stove, first moistening the polish with water, then rubbing the polish on with a cloth kept for such use. Then it is time to light the paper from under the grate, and while the fire is beginning to burn she polishes the stove with her dry brush. Here is something else to remember: blacken the stove while it is cold, but polish it as it begins to heat.

Watch well while the wood and coal are kindling, so as to be ready to add more coal as soon as it is necessary, since if you do not, it will refuse to kindle when you do put it on, and then you will have the fun — and it isn't such good fun either — of doing your work all over again. But if you give the necessary thought and care to it, you need never have this trouble. After your first coal has well kindled, you should add enough to come nearly to the top of the fire box, and then you may feel assured that everything is right. Here you see one of the homely old proverbs verified, " More haste, less speed."

You cannot make a coal fire at hap-hazard; you must go about it systematically. If you have charcoal or Franklin coal, it may be put on at first with the wood.

When the blue flame is no longer seen, close the oven damper; and as soon as the coal is burning freely, shut the front damper. Then regulate the fire by the slide or damper in the pipe. While making and watching the fire, empty the tea-kettle, wipe out the inside, fill it and the reservoir with fresh water — never fill either from the hot-water tank — doesn't it seem absurd to have to say this? — finish polishing the sides and back of the range, and brush up the hearth and floor.

Now we are ready for some cooking. But stop a minute; there is more to be said before that is begun. We must keep the fire, now it is made, and you will need some directions for that. So we will listen while the teacher gives them:

Somebody has said that it "takes a wise man to build a fire and a philosopher to keep it."

We have shown that it requires judgment if not real wisdom to get our fire well going, and certainly it requires thought to keep it. It needs attention, not in a fussy, but in a common-sense way. In the first place, one thing to be well borne in mind is that the coal should never come above the top of the lining of the fire box. It chokes the entrance to the oven channel, making it impossible for a steady heat to circulate freely there; and it spoils the stove by warping the covers and cracking them. So you see it is bad economy. The fuel is wasted and the stove is spoiled. If you need a steady hot fire for some time, replenish often and add but a little coal at a time.

If you do not need to use the fire, but wish to keep it along, add fresh coal, and when the gas is burned off, which will be as soon as the blue flame dancing over it disappears, close all the dampers, so there will be no draught, and your fire will keep a long time. When you wish to quicken your fire again after it has been closed a long time, open all the dampers, to give draughts to enliven it. If some of the coal remains black on the top, you may poke away the ashes underneath with the poker, then when it is burning add coal and shake it gently to clear the grate. But if the coal is red, then you must not poke it, or you will put it out. Add a few coals at a time, but not enough to choke it or cool it. When your first pieces are kindled add a few more, and when these are burning you may then venture to give a gentle shake or quiet poke to the fire, but be very careful that you do not shake or poke too much, lest you deaden your fire again, possibly putting it out altogether.

With all this instruction the teacher gives little lessons in chemistry, that are illustrated by the work that is done in the fire-building, and in this way the pupils are taught not only the how but the why; for you see in a thorough drill of this kind it is very important to "mind the whys and wherefores."

I think, after these explicit directions, any girl can build and keep a fire even if she hasn't been to the cooking school. And this is a very important lesson, you may be sure, because no other lesson can well be given until the fire-building is fully understood, for what good will all the rules for dishes do, if you haven't the fire to cook them by?

# CHAPTER III.

### SOME SIMPLE USES OF THE OVEN.

A SHORT time since the mother of a poor family died. The father was a hard-working sober man, and there were three children, the oldest a bright girl of thirteen. She had been a pupil in the Boston public cooking school for a year, and had been taught sewing since she entered the grammar department. When the mother died this young daughter stepped to the front, and took the housekeeping into her brave capable little hands. She kept the house tidy, the little children's clothes mended and clean, and she had always something well cooked for her father. She constantly surprised him with some special dish that was different from the ordinary food.

The father enjoyed it all, but he looked troubled and care-worn. One day, when she had cooked something particularly nice he praised it, then as if afraid of hurting her feelings he said, "I don't like to say anything, Mary, you are doing so nicely, but I am afraid we can't afford to have all these things. They are nice, but you must remember we are poor people."

Mary's hour of housekeeping triumph had come. "Indeed, father," she said, "it costs no more than the old way."

To prove it, she brought her little account-book, which she had kept very carefully, and showed him that she had not expended one cent over her allowance. The father was very proud and happy over his little daughter's achievement, and you may be sure he told all his acquaintances about it; and you may be sure also, that the industrial training in public schools has no more earnest advocate than this same man who has seen for himself the result of the training.

I tell this because it is always pleasant to know some of the practical good that comes of this kind of teaching, especially if you are inclined in any degree to advocate it. There will always be somebody sure to pop up and say, as so many do, "Yes, it is all very well to talk about the value of such training — but what has it ever done for anybody? We want the cold facts."

So here is one ready-made for use. It is not such a "cold" fact either, it is quite a heart-warming one.

Mary, with all the rest of the girls, learned how to make the fire, and to perform a housekeeper's duty. Next came a lesson in the simplest form of cooking — that of baking, or cooking by direct heat. The very first things the class was set to do was to bake potatoes, to prepare croûtons, and to brown bread-crumbs.

All this seems easy, doesn't it? Ah! but I would like to know how many of you can bake a potato perfectly, so that it shall be just mealy and white all through, with a crust that is not burned nor hardened. Tell me, now, are not the majority of baked potatoes that you see brought to the table so shrivelled and dried-up that half the contents are wasted, and the residue soggy and heavy? If that is not your experience it is mine; and as I particularly like baked potatoes, I don't mind putting on cap and apron, and coming to the class, hoping to find out something that I didn't know before.

The fire is built — there are no directions this time, for the fire-maker is supposed to have learned all about it at the last lesson. A few questions are asked to the remainder of the class, and if anything is done in the wrong place, or is omitted, the correction or the supplying the omission must come from the class. When the fire is built the lesson for the day begins.

The first step is baking without measurements or mixtures. Potatoes are cooked by themselves and do not require any combination with other ingredients. Select the potatoes of uniform size; that is so that all may be done at the same time. Should they vary in size, then some will be cooked before others, and these will burn or spoil while the others are cooking. Medium-sized potatoes are better for baking than either large or small. Having selected them, wash and scrub them well, so that the skins will be perfectly clean. Very many persons like to eat the skin of a baked potato, but it is not safe to do so unless you know they are thoroughly scrubbed, and are baked in a clean oven. That you must look out for as well. Do not place them directly upon the bottom of the oven, but upon the grate, which has been laid across the middle of the oven. The hot air gets all about them on every side, and they are cooked evenly. They must be baked until they are soft; this will take from half an hour to three quarters, according to the size of the potato, and the heat of the oven. When they are just done they will be plump, smooth and soft, and when opened they will be mealy. As soon as they are done break the skins to let the steam escape. It is this steam or gas that often makes a potato bitter when it is confined in the close skin for a long time, and it tends also to make the potato "soggy." Baked potatoes should be served at once, in an uncovered dish, as the steam that is generated in a covered dish will make them heavy. They can be warmed over as well as boiled potatoes; so if in cooking at home you have any left, peel them at once, as they will be in a better condition to warm over. No little thing betrays the unthrifty housekeeper more quickly than the habit of setting potatoes away unpeeled. Not only is much of the potato wasted when it is peeled after standing some time cold, but it cannot be prepared and served as daintily.

There is one thing that the school-training does, and that is to show girls the right way, and to prove that it is the best way. If only the girls who do not have the advantage of such training would take the hints that are given in these papers, they too might feel that they have achieved something, even without the school and the teacher. If a thing seems small to you, and of little significance, do not on that account neglect it, but remember that the sum of successful living is made up of an aggregate of trifles, and that each one must be scrupulously attended to, or the whole will go wrong. Isn't that a solemn sermon with a left-over baked potato for a text?

The next things are the croûtons. There is probably little need to explain that these are browned slices of bread to serve with soups or stews in place of toast. Sometimes they are fried, but now we are only just learning how to use the oven, and frying is ever so far away. The brown croûtons which the girls in the cooking class are preparing to make are very delicate and nice for the purpose for which they are used. The bread knives are got ready, the girls see that they are sharp, then slices half an inch thick are cut from the loaves of bread. The crusts are removed from these slices, and they are then cut into half-inch cakes, put into a shallow pan, set in the oven and baked until they are brown. But what becomes of the crusts? Are they thrown away? That would be waste, and waste is not tolerated in the class. Now is the time to give the first lesson in economy; in the thrift that made our grandmothers such wonderful housekeepers. And just here it is quite in order to say to the girls who are reading this, that the same use may be made of all bits of stale bread — no matter how small the pieces — that is being made of the crusts that were cut from the slices of bread for the croûtons. These are put into a pan and, when the oven is moderately hot so that there is no danger of the bread scorching, placed in the oven and heated until dry all through and crisp. Then remove the bread from the oven and roll it as fine as you possibly can. You will not be able to crush it uniformly, and some of the crumbs will be finer than the rest. It is best to separate the fine crumbs from the coarse, as they may be used advantageously for different purposes. To separate them, sift the crumbs, put the fine ones into one jar or bottle, the coarse ones into another, cork them and keep them in a dry place. They will keep a long time, and be a great convenience as they will be always ready for use. What will be done with them, do you ask? Well, they will be used for breading veal, lamb chops, oysters, or anything that is to be cooked in crumbs with beaten egg. By and by, when we come to it, you will be told how you are to use them; in the meantime you close them tight and put them where they will keep dry.

You see you have learned the simplest form of cooking, in which you have been given your fire and a simple article of food with no combination of ingredients. Now comes the next step. This is also baking, but with a little lesson in measuring and in preparation. Before going to work at the cooking there are some things to be learned that will prove valuable to you as long as you shall be called upon to cook, and you will be glad that you have learned them when it shall become your turn to teach. For that is going to happen surely. I wonder how many of you girls have ever thought of this: that when you are learning anything it is not for yourself alone; but that by and by you will be obliged to impart what you know to some one else. That is why the thoughtful women, who have had this training in charge, have given so much care to the best way of teaching the pupils. I am sure you will all see before we finish, that the methods are as natural as those employed in any science, and that every step is taken with reference, not only to the one that preceded it, but to all that are to follow. A great deal of wisdom and experience has gone into the planning of the course of training, and it is as nearly perfect as it is possible to be at the present.

But what is it you are to learn? It is something about measurements. You may all imagine, if you like, that with caps and aprons on, you are standing before your table while the teacher tells you the important things for you to remember. They are these:

Accurate measurement is necessary to insure success in cooking.

All dry materials should be sifted before measuring.

A cup holding just half a pint is the standard measuring cup.

A cupful is all the cup will hold without running over — full to the brim. A scant cupful is within a quarter of an inch of the top.

A tablespoonful of flour, sugar and butter is a rounded spoonful.

A teaspoonful of salt, pepper and spice, is a level teaspoonful.

A heaped spoonful is all the spoon will hold.

Half a spoonful is measured by dividing through the middle — lengthwise.

A speck is what you can take on the tip of a penknife.

Now we may go on and try a little baking with some simple combination of ingredients. It shall be baked apples. For these you will use to each apple one teaspoonful of sugar, and one tablespoonful of water. Pick out nice fair apples, unspecked and of uniform size. Wipe them nicely with a clean, dry cloth, remove the cores, and put them in an earthen dish. Put the sugar in the centre of each apple, in the cavity whence you have removed the core, and the water in the dish. Bake in a hot oven from twenty to thirty minutes, or until soft, but not until broken.

This is a good time to learn to brown crackers to serve with soups or oyster stews. For this you will use one half a teaspoonful of butter to each whole cracker. Split round crackers in halves, spread the inside with a thin layer of butter. Put them, buttered side uppermost, into a pan, and brown in a hot oven. Serve at once, and they will be found delightfully sweet and crisp.

A nice lunch dish is made of these same crackers, by preparing them in the way just given, then for every cracker mix one tablespoonful of grated cheese, one half a salt-spoonful of salt and one quarter of a salt-spoonful of pepper. Spread the hot crackers with this mixture of cheese and seasoning, return to the oven, and warm until the cheese is melted. Or you may make a brewis for tea by preparing the crackers and cheese in this way, putting them into a shallow earthen dish, adding a quarter of a cup of milk to each cracker, and baking until it is brown, or until the milk is absorbed.

Now this is all very easy, but, I assure you, it is nice, and will impart a relish for tea or luncheon that is inexpensive and easily prepared.

# CHAPTER IV.

### A LESSON IN BOILING.

THE little girls were folding up their aprons and putting away their caps after one of the lessons, and making ready to go home. I asked a bright miss of about twelve what she had learned.

"Oh!" she replied, "I have learned to make a fire and take care of it, to put away my things neatly after I am through my work, to look after my utensils and my towels, to bake potatoes and apples, and to make buns."

She told off the list of accomplishments with a pardonable air of pride.

"But you have learned to do these things here," I persisted; "have you done any of them at home?"

What a sparkle there was in the bright blue eyes!

"Yes, indeed," she said; "why, only this morning I took my mother's receipt-book and made the gems for breakfast by her rule. I not only mixed them, but I attended to the baking. I arranged the dampers, and no one but myself even looked at the oven once. My father said the gems were the nicest he ever tasted, and my mother said that was real cooking; that it was easy enough merely to mix things together, but the test of a good cook was in the baking."

And "mother" was right. Now I dare say all the lessons we have gone over have seemed very simple, and it may be that some of you are inclined to look with a little feeling of contempt on the small number of rules that have been given. But you must remember that we are learning principles, and that when these are well understood you can take any one's receipt-book and do anything you please, just as the little girl I have told you about made successful gems when she had learned how to manage her oven with such simple things as potatoes and apples.

I have a friend who is a very fine and very successful singing-teacher. He trains the voices of his pupils very carefully, with exercises that are best calculated to develop them. Now and again some pupil gets impatient over these exercises and begs to know when she can have a song to learn.

"When you know how to sing," is the invariable reply. "You must first know how to use your voice, then you may buy out the music store if you wish."

There it is again, you see; principles first, afterwards achievement. And so it is in everything, and so it must be. Theories are very fine, no doubt, but they do not always take the place of principles. Not very many days ago, I was reading one of the many theoretical articles that are written on the subject of housekeeping. The writer in advising housekeepers how to keep ahead of their work, said that every night before retiring, the fire in the kitchen stove should be laid for the morning, and the tea-kettle filled. Fancy using water for tea or coffee or cocoa that has stood in a kettle for twelve hours. Why, any housekeeper, no matter how inexperienced she was, would know better, and certainly every schoolgirl would, after she had taken the present lesson on boiling.

We have a fashion of speaking about boiling food, such as potatoes, and other vegetables, grains and some meats. Now the proper way would be to speak of them as cooked in boiling water; the articles themselves do not boil, only the water in which they are cooked. Baking is cooking by a dry heat; boiling is cooking in a boiling liquid. This is one of the most common forms of cooking, and the liquid that is most usually employed is water. By trying experiments with the water, that is, by watching it as it boils and testing it to find the temperature — these facts are discovered:

COOKING IN BOILING WATER.

That water boils at 212°, or when it bubbles all over the top. That when once it boils all over it will become no hotter, and that fuel and heat are wasted when it boils at a galloping rate. This is a very good thing to know, because many people imagine that the more furiously anything boils, the hotter it gets and the more rapidly it cooks. That is a false notion, as you can tell by testing the water during boiling by a thermometer that is made on purpose for testing the heat of liquids. So here is something that it is well, in the interests of economy, to remember.

The kettle should never be so full that the water will boil over as it expands in heating. There is danger of injuring the stove if this is allowed, and, too, there is always danger of somebody getting scalded, which is, as you probably know, the most painful of all ways of burning the flesh.

You find too, what so many people who cook forget to remember—that there is a wide distinction between "boiled water" and "boiling water," and that the freshness is lost by long boiling, so that the sooner water is used after once boiling the better it will be. Indeed if it stands it loses all its vitality, and cannot be used with good results. That is why tea and coffee are often so lifeless; not because the leaves and berries are not good, but because they are improperly made with "boiled water" instead of freshly "boiling water." You see there is a wide distinction between the two.

The lesson in boiling takes up the boiling of vegetables, potatoes being taken as the demonstrating article. The principles for cooking all vegetables are the same, and if the pupil learns to cook one kind well, she can, by following the particular directions, cook any kind as occasion may require. As in baking, select the potatoes for boiling of a uniform size. This is to insure all being cooked at a time. Wash and scrub them. Pare, and cover with cold water. Put them in boiling salted water, using one quart of water and one tablespoonful of salt for six large potatoes. Cook until done, which will be in half an hour or a trifle over. Drain off every drop of water. Place the kettle, uncovered, at the back of the stove to let the water pass off in steam. Shake gently, and serve the potatoes very hot.

Potatoes, when pared, turn brown if exposed to the air, and each should be covered with cold water as soon as pared, and should not be pared long before using. If they are left, even a short time, uncovered after paring, the action of the air will turn them brown, and they will not lose this discoloration in the cooking, so they are not so appetizing. They should be taken up the moment they are done; this is one of the most important steps of all. When a fork will pierce them easily they are ready; drain them, too, at once.

And now, since some of you may like to vary your plain boiled potato, we will see what else may be done with it, and how it may be served to be more tempting. Of course there is always "mashed potato," which is very nice when well prepared, and not at all good when carelessly done. It is like so many simple things; a little more thought and a trifle more labor, turn into success what might prove a failure. To one pint of hot boiled potatoes, add one tablespoonful of butter, one half teaspoonful of salt, a dust of pepper, and enough hot milk to moisten. Mash in the sauce-pan in which they were boiled; beat with a fork until light and creamy, then turn out carefully and lightly into a hot dish.

Sometimes there is mashed potato left over, and it can be made very nice for breakfast by using it for potato cakes, which are prepared in the following way: Make the cold mashed potato into small round cakes about one half an inch thick. Put them on a baking tin, and brush them over with milk; then bake in a hot oven until the cakes are a golden brown.

If you like a more ornamental dish than you

will get with simple mashed potato, you may, when the potatoes are mashed and beaten and seasoned, rub them with a wooden masher through a strainer into a hot dish and then you will have "rice potatoes."

Having learned how to cook the potatoes by boiling, you can undertake other vegetables, but there are some general rules that you may first learn. And first about the preparation, which is always important.

Potatoes: scrub and pare when necessary. It is not always necessary to pare new potatoes, and the thin, delicate skin, not yet grown tough, will come off by rubbing.

Parsnips: scrub till white, and trim off the fine, threadlike roots.

Carrots: scrub, and scrape off the thin outer surface.

Turnips: scrub, cut in slices and pare.

Beets: wash carefully, for if the skin be broken the sugary juices will escape.

Cabbage and cauliflower: trim and soak, top down, to draw out any insects.

Celery: wash and scrape off any rusty portions.

Spinach and other greens: pick over very carefully, and wash in several waters.

Onions: peel and soak.

Green corn: husk with clean hands, but do not wash it.

Peas and beans: shell with clean hands and wash quickly.

Soft-shell squashes: wash, pare, and cut as desired.

Hard-shell squashes: wash, split, and cook in the shell.

Asparagus: wash, and break off the tough ends, tie in bundles, and break into inch bits.

String beans: strip off the ends and strings on each side, cut or break into small pieces and wash.

Fresh vegetables do not require any soaking in cold water, and it is better not to prepare them until you are ready to cook them. But if they are wilted, soaking will freshen them, and if they must be prepared long before cooking, they should be covered with cold water to prevent them from wilting or from becoming discolored.

For all fresh green vegetables use soft water, salted and freshly boiling. Cook rapidly until soft. The time will depend upon the age or freshness of the vegetable.

With green peas, shelled beans, green corn, asparagus, celery and spinach, use as little water as possible, and let it boil away, leaving just enough to moisten and thus save all the desirable soluble matter that may have been drawn out.

Cook cabbage and cauliflower uncovered, in a large kettle of rapidly-boiling, salted water, with a salt-spoonful of soda in it.

Onions, scald and change the water twice.

All others, cook in water enough to cover, and drain it off after cooking.

Green summer squash, cabbage and other watery vegetables should be pressed in a cloth or strainer, and well drained.

And now the ways of preparing the vegetables being quite understood, the next thing in order is the time of cooking. The following formula for boiling meats and other things besides vegetables, is given the pupils to learn.

| | |
|---|---|
| Eggs (soft), coffee, clams, oysters | 3 to 5 minutes |
| Green corn, small fish and thin slices of fish | 5 to 10 " |
| Rice, sweet breads, peas, tomatoes, asparagus, hard boiled eggs | 15 to 20 " |
| Potatoes, macaroni, squash, celery, spinach, cabbage | 20 to 30 " |
| Young beets, carrots, turnips, onions, parsnips, cauliflower | 30 to 45 " |
| String beans, shelled beans, oyster plant | 45 to 60 " |
| Winter vegetables, oatmeal, hominy and wheat, chickens and lamb | 1 to 2 hours |
| Fowls, turkey, veal | 2 to 3 " |
| Corned beef, smoked tongue, beef á la mode | 3 to 4 " |

| | |
|---|---|
| Ham | 4 to 5 hours |
| Small pieces of meat, allow fifteen minutes to warm through, then for every pound | 15 minutes |
| Halibut and salmon, in cubical form, per pound | 15 " |
| Blue fish, bass, etc., per pound | 10 " |
| Cod, haddock and small fish per pound | 6 " |

For the benefit of the mothers who may think either I or the cooking school have gone astray on the matter of cooking cabbage, I want to emphasize here the advantage of the new way over the old. I was as sceptical over the notion of cabbage being properly cooked in half an hour, as any one of you can be; but my first experiment corrected me, and all who tasted this maligned vegetable served after the new method declared themselves surprised.

Have plenty of salted, boiling water, in which a teaspoonful of soda has been dissolved, plunge the cabbage in, top downward, leave it uncovered and let it boil until tender, that will be, as given in the time table, from twenty minutes to half an hour. Take it out into a colander, drain well, put into a hot dish, put in bits of butter, some salt and pepper, and serve at once. It will be as delicate as cauliflower; the color will be retained and there will not be an unpleasant odor over the house, such as is always associated with boiling cabbage. Try it once, and then see if the School Kitchen Learning has not gotten several steps in advance of your old, traditional methods.

And now for the seasoning after once the vegetables are cooked. One pint of vegetables, mashed or sliced, or one pint of small whole vegetables requires one tablespoonful of butter, one half teaspoonful of salt, and one half saltspoonful of pepper. Squash, peas and beans are improved by one teaspoonful of sugar. Milk or the vegetable liquid may be used to moisten such as are too dry.

Eggs come naturally into a lesson in boiling, and so the way for doing them is given. For soft-boiled eggs, you will put the eggs in a saucepan, cover with boiling water, and let them stand from six to ten minutes where the water will keep hot, but not boiling. The white will be soft and jelly-like and the yolk soft but not liquid. Eggs cooked in this manner are really "coddled eggs," but they will be found as nice, and more digestible, than when cooked in the usual fashion. Or if one prefers the white hardened while the yolk remains soft, the eggs may be cooked in boiling water about three minutes. If you wish the eggs hard boiled cook for twenty minutes in water just bubbling. The yolk will be dry and mealy and adjustable, where if it is cooked only ten minutes it will simply be hard and tough, and will not digest easily. Try these for yourself and see.

# CHAPTER V.

### GOING TO MARKET.

THE next lesson in cap and apron is on cooking meats; but before the meats are cooked they must be bought; and it is quite important that the cooks should know how to buy them. It is all very well to order hap-hazard of one's provision-man, but how is one to know whether she gets what she orders unless she has learned the different cuts of meat, where they are situated, and what she ought to pay for them?

So one day the school kitchen is deserted, and the class is taken by the teacher down to the big markets, and there they are initiated into the mysteries of rumps and rounds and loins, of shoulders and fillets, of briskets and rattle rounds, of ribs and flanks, of saddles and shins, and the rest of the long list of cuts, which all their lives they have heard talked about, without understanding or knowing one part from another.

Of course if one is going to be a good housekeeper one must know what to buy, and how to make the best use of what she buys. She must learn, too, to do her marketing according to the needs of her family. If she is providing for persons who do a great deal of out-of-door work she will want the heavier kinds of food. If for persons who are in-doors a great deal and whose work is sedentary, she will want to provide lighter food. Whether light or heavy it must be nourishing, but it will differ in quality.

In the buying of meat a lesson in economy is given. And now, my young housekeepers in prospective, don't turn up your noses at this word, and above all, don't get a wrong idea of the meaning of the term. The notion that prevails the most popularly is a very mistaken one. I have had occasion to talk about this very thing to older people than you, and I have found that pretty nearly all of them had fallen into the same fault. Now please remember this — it is the very same thing I told them — economy does not imply meanness. It is only another word for good, honest thrift. It means doing the very best you possibly can with the money at your command. It is a moral obligation. It is care-taking in its best and highest sense. You will have respect for the word as soon as you settle it in your mind that it is not by any means connected with stinginess. So in learning about meats and the way to buy them to the best advantage, you are learning "economy" because you are taking lessons in wisdom of selection, and the ways to get the most good with the money you have to use. You will learn, too, when the different meats are in season, which is needed knowledge, as you will find when you come to be put to the test.

The first part of the lesson at the stall is about beef, and the market-man, who has come to know the bright-faced, eager-eyed girls very well, and evidently has an unbounded admiration for the teacher, has put down upon the table half a beef, and as the teacher explains he cuts, in order to show the different pieces as she names them. They have already taken a preliminary lesson from the diagram at the school, but it is more satisfactory to see the meat — they understand it much better.

Good beef, the teacher tells them, should be bright-red when it is first cut, and this red flesh should be well marbled with yellowish fat, and there should be a thick layer of fat on the outside. If it does not present this appearance, it is safe to assume that the ox was not well-fatted, was too young, or was not in good condition. All these things one can see for herself; by them she will know when the beef is good. Also she is told that the flesh should be firm, and no mark should be left when it is pressed with the finger. The suet should be dry and crumble easily.

The first thing that is to be done, is to

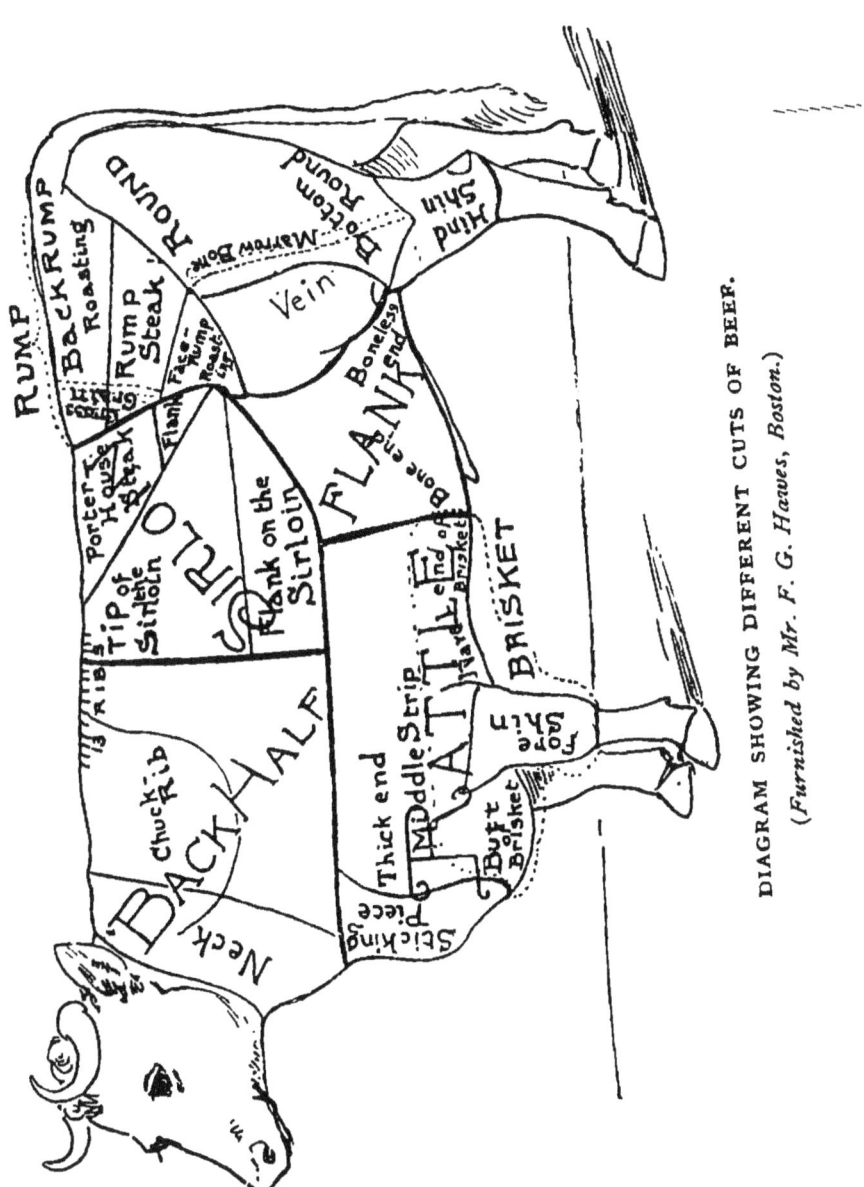

DIAGRAM SHOWING DIFFERENT CUTS OF BEEF.

(Furnished by Mr. F. G. Hawes, Boston.)

divide the beef into the hind and fore-quarters. The hind-quarter contains the finest and most expensive cuts of the meat. Here are found the sirloin, the tenderloin, the rump and the round. The cheapest portions of the hind-quarter are the shin and the flank. In the fore-quarter are the ribs, the shoulder, the shin, the rattle round and the brisket. The ribs are the top of the back nearest to the loin, join it, in fact, when the animal is whole. The first five ribs are what are called the "prime" ribs; these are used for roasts or steaks; the next are the five chock ribs lying between the prime ribs and the neck; the meat is of a finer quality than on the "prime" ribs, although they are used for the same purposes. The neck is used for beef teas, for stews, and for boiling. Below the rib-cuts, running along the side of the animal, is the rattle round. This is used for corning. The under part of the animal's body is called the brisket, and this is also used for corning. The shoulder is used for steaks and corning, though the less said about the tenderness of a shoulder steak the better. The shin, both in the front and the back, is used for soups and soup-stock.

In the hind-quarter come the first roasts and steaks, as well as the juciest meats for making beef tea, meat pies, beef à la mode or potted beef. Sirloin, of course, gives the very choicest roasts and steaks; next comes the rump; this is cut in three parts. The back, the middle and the face are good roasting pieces; but the most economical is the middle cut, as it is free from bone, and has not a scrap of waste on it. Good steaks are cut from the top of the round; some people go so far as to say that the flavor of a round steak is superior to that of any other. The lower portion of the round is used for braising and for beef tea.

The tenderloin has the most tender meat, but it is neither so juicy nor so well-flavored as other portions that are not so tender, and it is not nearly so nutritious as portions that require much cooking. The sirloin comes next in tenderness and delicacy. These cost more than any other cuts, but there is less nutritive value than is found in the cheaper parts. Indeed the cost of the meat seems to be in an inverse ratio to its real food-value. Of course this is so because of the much smaller proportion of the so-called choicer cuts. It is one of the wise economies of nature that it should be so. The harder-working class of people, those who do a great deal of manual labor, and particularly those whose occupation takes them a great deal into the open air, need the nourishment and sustaining quality of the heavier meats. And these are found in the cheaper parts, particularly where there is a great deal of juice in the meat and rich marrow in the bone. Stews, and braised meats, or those that are steamed in their own juices over the fire, as pot-boiled meats, give the most nutriment, and add the physical strength that is needed, as well as in cold weather supplying a deal of warmth by furnishing the carbon for the body.

In this last cause is found the reason why one

cares less for food of this kind in the summer. Stimulation and heat are to be avoided when the weather is warm, and that is why vegetables nd fish are more palatable in the summer than n the colder weather. One very important point to be learned is how one is to vary the foods to suit the seasons, and so come as nearly as possible to an ideal diet. It is not within the jurisdiction of these papers to dwell much upon these points, but perhaps the few hints given now and then will set you all thinking, and perhaps send you to the proper sources for all the necessary information.

Mutton, like beef, is good all the year round, and the younger it is the more delicate. Still the nicer meat is gotten from a larger animal, and there should be a good deal of flesh on the bones. For buying lamb or mutton you may have the saddle, or the whole hind-quarter, the leg, loin, and shoulder. The saddle is roasted; the leg is roasted or boiled; the loin is roasted or cut into chops; and the shoulder is roasted.

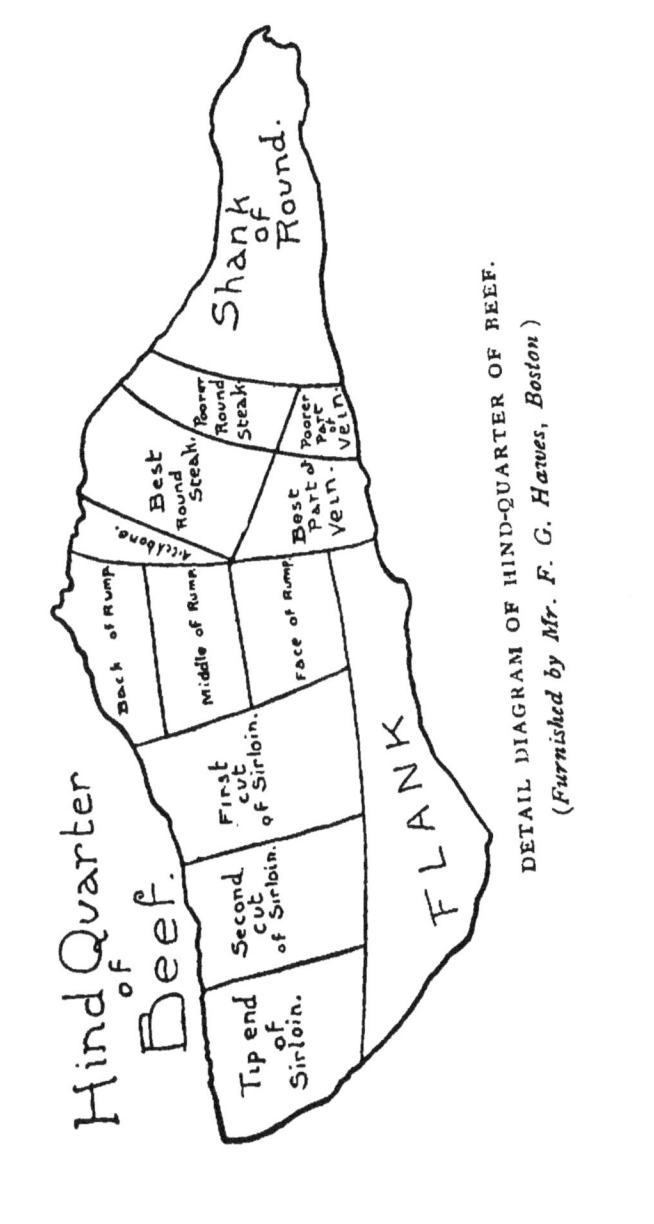

DETAIL DIAGRAM OF HIND-QUARTER OF BEEF.
(*Furnished by Mr. F. G. Hawes, Boston.*)

The hind-quarter costs more than the fore-quarter; but the shoulder-piece, boned and stuffed, makes a very nice and inexpensive roast. The shoulder and neck piece are also used for lamb stews and fricassees.

Chops are cut two ways; there is the long chop and the short chop. The long chop has the flank-end left on, while in the short chop it is cut off and only the loin-part left. The long chop costs less by the pound, but really it is no cheaper since the flank-piece adds to the weight, and there is but very little meat on it. It takes so much more to make the amount needed, that in the end it costs about as much as the lesser number of pounds of short chops.

The heart and liver of beef are both used for food, and the heart of mutton. The liver is either broiled or braised, and the heart is braised.

Only by experience can one learn to tell exactly the cuts when she sees them, and it would be a good thing if after the lesson on marketing the mothers would trust the daughters to buy some of the family supplies of meat, thus giving them the opportunity to put this lesson into practise. Of course they would begin with the cheaper prices, in which there is little risk, and every time they made a selection it would be an added lesson. Almost every family has its own market-man, and when he saw the interest, he would no doubt give the little purchaser a great deal of valuable information, thus supplementing what her teacher has given in this marketing lesson. There is no danger in putting a certain amount of responsibility upon a child; it makes her careful and thoughtful, and gives her a certain discretion that is a valuable addition to the character. I don't mean to make a little prig of her, for no one dislikes a prig worse than I, but a young girl can be thoughtful and useful and discreet without being priggish, and without losing any of the sweet youthfulness that is so desirable.

## CHAPTER VI.

### MEATS AND MADE-OVERS.

"CHOPPING IT FINE."

DID you ever notice what a little thing it takes, sometimes, to set the whole current of a life in a certain direction? Sometimes it is so slight that we cannot see it, and then we talk about "happenings," just as though anything in the world ever merely happened. All this comes of a visit one of the mothers of a girl, graduated the year before, made to the teacher of the cooking school. She said, "I could not help coming to tell you what the cooking class means for my daughter."

She was a colored woman who had been a cook in a Southern family, but had married and come to Boston, where she had brought up a family of children, giving them the benefit of a public school training. All this she told the teacher. Then she said:

"My daughter was very much interested in the cooking, and I used to let her try her lessons over at home. I was delighted with what she did, because not only was the food that she cooked good, but she did it in such a nice handy way. Last Sunday I let her cook all the dinner, and I'll tell you what she had. Roast goose and apple sauce, mashed potatoes, squash, turnips, and apple pie. Every thing was so good. We had company, and they didn't stop praising Ada all day. I tell you I was prouder than she was, and she was proud enough. She just loves it, and now I'll tell you what I'm going to do. I'm going to send her through the Normal School, then I want her to go through the Normal Cooking School, then go South and teach her people. She's just wild to do it, and now we're going straight ahead because we know just what we're working for, thanks to you, and the ladies who started the school."

It is a good thing to have one's vocation fixed, so as to know "just what one is working for," isn't it? I think Mrs. Hemenway will be glad she was impelled to start this movement, even for this one girl's sake, whose future lies before her, a straight path clearly cut.

In the subject of this chapter we have a full day's work; work for two classes, and this is the way it is managed in the school. The lesson for "meats" comes in the morning, the lesson on "made-overs" in the afternoon. This is because the meat being cooked in the first lesson it is ready for use in the second, so the same material really does service for both lessons and a saving is made in this way. For you must see that unless a great deal of care is exercised, the expenses of providing material for so many to work with, might easily be increased so that the outlay would exceed the appropriation. This would never do; for one of the first things to be learned is how to make the sum in hand cover all the expense of buying. Of course this is a matter that must rest with the teacher; but in preparing the course of instruction Miss Homans was very particular in having every thing tested, and every expense brought down to the lowest figure. In this she was admirably seconded by Miss Hope the teacher of the Tennyson Street School, and it is that system, tested and well proven, that is the basis of all the teaching in the schools of Boston and vicinity; and, indeed, of all the schools which have sprung from the Boston experiment. I shall have something to say about the expenses of a year's work later, as well as something about the Normal Training, and the kind of teachers that are required to make this work a success.

But to come back to our lessons: as one class comes only half a day at a time, it becomes quite evident that the class which learns about meat in the morning isn't the one that has to take the instruction about made-over dishes in the afternoon and *vice versa*. But every girl must have all the lessons, so these two are repeated for the next day and the classes are changed about. The one that learned about meats comes in the afternoon, and takes the lesson in made-overs, and the class that was the afternoon class before is the morning class this time. So you see all get the instruction, and the cost of the four lessons is put into the cost of two; a little household management, such as you all will have to put into practise one day or other, and it is just as well to take your lesson early.

There are many ways of cooking meat, roasting, boiling, braising, broiling, and frying or sautéeing. The ways of cooking depends upon the pieces of meat that are to be cooked. If the fibers are tough it should be boiled or braised. It is the tender meat only which can be either roasted or broiled to be palatable, comfortably eaten and well-digested.

One of the simplest ways of preparing meat is to boil it. The piece to be boiled should be well wiped, then put at once into boiling water that has been salted. The water should cover the meat, and it should boil for a few minutes, when it may be set back on the fire, and simmer gently until the meat is done. If the water is boiling when the meat is put in. the intense heat sears the surface and prevents the juice of the meat from flowing out and wasting, and the meat when done is juicy and well-flavored, having lost very little in the process of cooking. During the boiling a scum arises to the surface, and this should be carefully removed; the kettle should be kept covered except when it is uncovered for skimming the surface of the water, as the steam assists greatly in softening the tough fibers, and the flavor is also better preserved.

It would escape into the air with the steam if it were not kept in.

The length of time that the meat should be boiled depends upon its weight. It takes about twenty minutes for the heat to pierce through a piece of meat so that it is ready to begin to cook; reckoning from that time, twelve or fifteen minutes should be allowed to a pound. If the meat is cut thick the longer time will be required; but if it is a flat, thin piece, the shorter time will be found sufficient.

Roasting meat is, properly, cooking it before the open fire, by subjecting it to a high degree of heat; but as this is rarely done in these days of ranges and cooking stoves we bake it in a hot oven and call it "roasted" by courtesy.

Braising is cooking in the oven in a covered pan, smothering the meat in its own juices and having a good deal of seasoning in the dish with the meat.

Broiling is cooking directly over hot coals, and is the quickest, as well as the hottest way of cooking. In nothing is the article to be cooked subjected to such an intense heat as in this process, and it would be quickly burned if the cook did not see to it that it was turned very often. I sometimes think that the majority of people who broil a beefsteak think they must do it literally. I suppose those of you who are French scholars know that the word comes from the French word *bruler*, "to burn;" it also means "to sear," and that is what should be done, the surface seared — not burned — so that all the juices shall be kept inside the meat. Turning it frequently, so that the surface shall cook and not burn, and in this way keeping the juices flowing from side to side, but not escaping, is the true way of making a successful broiled dish. Food cooked in this way should be served at once, on hot plates, from a hot platter.

This much in a general way. I think you will understand from the above, what are the underlying principles of the various processes, and why they are practised. Now for some of the particular rules. We will suppose that you are ready to begin, and that you are to boil a leg of mutton for dinner. You will wipe the meat, remove all the fat, and put the meat into boiling, salted water, after you have weighed it. Allow ten or fifteen minutes for the heat to penetrate the meat, taking the longer time for a large piece; then skim off whatever may have risen to the top of the water, set the kettle back where the water will simmer, and cook in this way until the meat is done, allowing twelve minutes to each pound. Serve it with parsley or caper sauce. The latter is usually preferred with mutton. To make this sauce or gravy, the following rule will be used. To each cup of boiling water in which the mutton was cooked, add one teaspoonful of flour moistened with a little cold water, one teaspoonful of vinegar, one half a saltspoonful of salt and a speck of pepper. Boil five minutes stirring constantly until smooth, then add one tablespoonful of capers, or of finely chopped parsley.

I think boiled mutton is as easy a dinner to begin with as any meat dish I know of. My own little eleven-year-old daughter came to me one day, when it chanced that the cook had taken a day to visit some friends, and begged to be allowed to cook the dinner. I had planned for something else, but remembering that the mutton was in the cold closet, I got it out and gave her the directions. She followed them implicitly, and with the tyranny for which cooks are famous forbade me the kitchen. So I was compelled to give directions from the library, and Missy got all the dinner, including vegetables and a rice pudding which was stuffed very full of plums to meet Missy's notion and papa's taste. Of course I enjoyed the dinner, and need I tell you that I felt very proud of the little body who had been so glad and proud in helping "mamma" through a very busy morning? And let me whisper here, there is a sequel to this dinner which I will tell you about farther on.

And now for the lesson in roasting. Suppose we take a calf's heart, and make a dish which for economy and delicacy is not half well enough known, although it will be after a few hundred more girls have learned how to prepare it. You must wash the heart thoroughly in cold water, to remove the blood, and cut out the veins and arteries. This may not be a pleasant task to every one, still it is no more unpleasant than preparing fowls or game. Make a stuffing with one tablespoonful of bread crumbs, one tablespoonful of chopped onions, one saltspoonful of powdered sage, one half a saltspoonful of salt, and a tiny bit of pepper. This you may moisten with milk or water. After it is prepared put it into the cavity caused by the removal of the arteries, and sew the edges together. Slice an onion and brown it in a tablespoonful of clarified dripping; skim out the pieces of onion, reserving them for use, brown the heart in the seasoned fat, then put it with the onion in a deep dish, and half cover with boiling water. Bake in a hot oven one hour, basting every ten minutes, add more water if necessary. When the heart is done you may make a gravy by thickening the water that is left in the dish with a little flour wet in cold water, just as you did in the mutton gravy. You will find this a very nice occasional dish for dinner, and a very inexpensive one.

You will observe that the rule gives clarified drippings as a proper fat for browning the onion and meat. You will, perhaps, like to know how the fat is clarified. Save any pieces of fat — excepting mutton — cut into half-inch cubes, and put them in a pan, covering them with cold water. Put the pan in the oven and cook slowly for four or five hours, or until the scraps are quite brown and the water evaporated. Slices of raw potato put in with the fat, also assist in the clarifying. When it is slightly cooled, but not beginning to harden, strain into an earthen jar or bowl and set aside for use.

And now suppose you wish to cook a beefsteak for breakfast. You will wipe the slice with a clean damp cloth — always, you see, this must be done with all meat, for you do not know what hands may have touched it — reserve the superfluous fat, and the bone. Grease the bars of the gridiron with some of the fat. Broil over a clear fire, not letting the gridiron out of your hands, and turning every time you count ten. If you like your steak rare cook it about four minutes, that is if it is of the right thickness, which is from three quarters of an inch to one inch; but taking a longer time if you wish it well done. Serve at once on a hot platter, and season with salt, butter, and a little pepper. You must give your undivided attention to steak if you wish it good. In fact its price, like that of liberty, is "eternal vigilance."

There is another way of broiling, that is called "pan broiling." This is done in a frying-pan or on a griddle. It is heated hissing hot, the meat is put on it, without any fat, cooked one minute, then turned the other side round, then cooked until done, turning very often. When properly done it has the flavor of steak or chops cooked over the coals.

And now for some of the ways of warming over the meats; preparing the "made-overs" or *réchauffés*, as the French call them. We will suppose we have some of our boiled mutton left. I will give you three ways in which you may use it. First is minced mutton on toast. Remove all the fat and gristle from the cold mutton, and chop it fine. To one cup of the meat, add one saltspoonful of salt, a speck of pepper, and one half a cup of the thickened gravy. Heat quickly in a saucepan, and pour over slices of toast. Serve hot.

The second way is a "cottage pie," and this, by the way, the cooking-school girls are very fond of doing at home. Prepare the meat as for the minced mutton or toast. Boil and mash some potatoes — you have already learned how to do that; to every cup of meat add one half a saltspoonful of salt, a bit of pepper, a little nutmeg — or if preferred a teaspoonful of chopped onion — and one half a cup of gravy. Put the meat, seasoning and gravy in a pie dish, cover it with mashed potato and bake in the oven until the potato is a golden brown.

Next comes scalloped mutton. Cut the cold mutton into small thin pieces, removing all the fat and gristle. Put a layer of bread crumbs in the bottom of a shallow baking dish, then a layer of meat, a very thin layer of crumbs, then gravy. Alternate these layers until the dish is full, spread buttered crumbs on the top and bake until the crumbs are brown.

# CHAPTER VII.

### SOUPS AND STEWS.

IN talking with the English-trained teacher of one of the cooking schools, she said that very early in her American experience she was struck with the absence of soup from the tables of the ordinary American family.

"It seems to me," she said, "that here in America you regard soup as a luxury, and leave it entirely to the rich people, putting out of sight the fact that it is one of the most nourishing and least expensive forms of food. Now can you tell me why it is?"

I told her what I really thought, what I have found indeed to be the fact: that people do not at all regard it from any economical standpoint; that they have grown to think the making of soup involves a deal of labor — which is quite a mistaken notion, as our white-capped and aproned girls quickly learn. To be sure there is a little more work in making a soup than in leaving it unmade ; but it is one of the things that pay for themselves, and after all, the dread of it is much greater than the doing.

But a prominent feature of the School-Kitchen work is the preparation of soups, both with and without stock, and the cooking of savory stews. And how good they both are, when one comes home with a keen appetite after a morning at school ! The odor is enough to make a hungry boy or girl hungrier than ever. There is nothing I like better than going to the school when I know they are learning in this special line of cookery.

Let us go together to-day to Tennyson street, and take the lesson in soup and stew-making. Caps and aprons are on, the "cutting boards" are taken out from under desks and tables and laid upon them, and knives are examined to see if they are sharp. The "cutting board" is a small board that is like a bread-board in miniature, and is used to cut meat upon, thus protecting the work-table. You will find that it is much easier to wash a small board like that, than to have your whole table to scour. These little economies of time and labor are among the most valuable of the things that are taught in the School Kitchen — just ask your mother if they are not; she has probably learned their worth by this time.

Now comes the explanation of the difference between a soup and a stew. In the first, the object is to extract all the goodness and the nourishing qualities from the meat, and having seasoned this extract properly to serve it in its liquid form. The simple, plain extract of the meat, when it is prepared, is called "stock," and it serves as a basis for several kinds of soup. For instance: if you add to your headstock bits of macaroni that have been boiled in salted water, then cut into short pieces, you have a macaroni soup; if you add carrot, turnip and other vegetables cut in small dice or fanciful designs, you have a Julienne soup; if you add barley you have "barley soup;" if you clear the stock and serve it plain you have a consommé. But in them all the stock or basis is the same.

You will see from the pieces of meat that the teacher places before you, that she has not selected the finest and the most expensive cuts, but that she has taken the coarser, heavier parts, with a good deal of bone. Listen, and she will tell you why.

"These pieces," she says, "are not available for roasting or broiling, yet they are full of nutriment, and are more strengthening than the finer cuts. We must use them in some way; it will not do to throw away the best part of the beef. So we extract the nourishment and make it into a soup. The way to get all the strength from the meat is to put it — after cutting it into small pieces and cracking the bones — into a kettle and cover it with cold water; letting it stand a little while on the back of the stove or range, then bringing it forward where it will heat very slowly."

What you will want for the stock is the following list of ingredients: Two pounds of the hind-shin of beef, two quarts of salt water, six whole cloves, six peppercorns, one bunch of sweet-herbs, one blade of mace not more than an inch long, two teaspoonfuls of salt, one small onion, half of a small carrot, half of a small turnip, one sprig of parsley. The herbs are sage, savory, marjoram, thyme and bay. If you are buying them for yourself, buy the whole herbs, dried, and not the sifted ones put into boxes. You don't know exactly what you are getting in these boxes, but you may feel pretty sure that it is something beside what you are paying for. If you are where you can have a bit of ground, just have your own herb-bed. But I shall have something more to say about that another time, so I won't stop for anything but the suggestion now.

The ingredients are together now, and the real

work begins. Wipe the meat carefully and cut it in small pieces, break the bone, and put meat, bones and marrow into the soup kettle; cover with the cold water and let it soak for half an hour or so, while you are preparing the vegetables. Stick the cloves into the onion, put a tablespoonful of butter or clear beef dripping into a sauce pan and set it over the gas stove; brown the onion in this, being very careful not to burn it; cut the carrot and turnip fine; then add them, the browned onion, the spices and herbs, to the meat and water. You will let this simmer if possible for five or six hours. Perhaps some one says that the session of the school will not be long enough to allow of giving this time to it. I will tell you how they manage in the School Kitchen. The class that comes in the morning prepares the soup and puts it over to cook, and it is finished by the class which comes in the afternoon. The lessons are repeated the next week when the classes are changed, so that the afternoon class gets the morning lessons of the week before, and the morning class in its turn gets the afternoon lessons, so that each class has the entire process of soup-making.

When the soup is sufficiently cooked, strain it through a fine strainer, over which you have laid a piece of strainer-cloth. Then set it aside to cool. When you wish to use it, take off the hard cake of fat which has formed on the top, and you will find beneath a thick, rich jelly, which is the stock or basis of any soup in the list of brown soups you may choose to make.

I have already told you how by using different materials with this stock you may vary your soup. I will now give you one or two rules for special soups taught at the school.

Take first rice soup, which is a great favorite. To make this, you will use the materials in the following proportions: to every cup of stock allow one half tablespoonful of rice and one salt-spoonful of salt; cook the rice in boiling salted water for half an hour, or until it is tender, then drain it and add it to the boiling stock.

For the mixed vegetable or (as it is called on hotel bills-of-fare) Julienne soup: to every cup of stock one tablespoonful each of carrot and turnip, and the usual saltspoonful of salt; wash and scrape the carrot, pare the turnip, and cut them both into tiny dice about a quarter of an inch square, put them into boiling salted water and cook them until they are tender, drain them, and add them to the boiling stock to which the salt has been previously added. It probably is unnecessary to tell you that all soups should be served hot — nothing is more depressing to the stomach or mind than half-chilled soup.

Now a word about soups without stock; these are made from vegetables, enriched by the addition of butter, milk and cream, and savory by the judicious addition of seasonings. Indeed one of the first things you will be taught in the School Kitchen, is the value of herbs and spices as related to food. If any one were to ask me the secret of good cooking, I should say " seasoning first, seasoning last, and seasoning all the time." It is this that makes food palatable and enjoyable.

The simplest of these soups without stock, as well as one of the most nourishing, is the potato soup; it it also inexpensive and easily prepared. The proportions and ingredients are as follows: for every three potatoes use one pint of milk, or if milk is not easily obtainable and you are obliged to be sparing of it, you may use one half pint of milk and one half pint of water; one tablespoonful of chopped onion, one teaspoonful of salt, a speck of white pepper — you will find out how much " a speck " is by referring back to your table of measurements that was given in one of the earlier chapters — one half tablespoonful of flour, one half tablespoonful of dripping or butter; unless the butter is very good use clear beef dripping in preference. So much for the ingredients ; now for the soup. Wash and pare the potatoes and cook them in boiling water until they are soft ; while the potatoes are cooking put the milk over in the double-

PARSLEY AND THYME.

boiler with the onion. When the potatoes are done drain and mash them, add the boiling milk and the seasoning, rub them through a strainer, put them back in the double-boiler to boil again. Then melt the dripping in a small saucepan, add the flour, stirring it constantly as it thickens. When the flour is well cooked, which will be in three or four minutes, add it to the boiling soup, stirring it well in; letting it boil five minutes, add one tablespoonful of finely chopped parsley and serve it hot, with croûtons which you learned to make in the chapter on baking.

I have given so much time to soups that I am afraid I cannot say as much as I would like about stews, but I will have time to tell you enough so that you, like the girls in the School Kitchen, may dare to try to make a simple stew at home.

In a soup all the nutriment of the meat is extracted, and it is served in the liquid form; in making stews the goodness of the meat is to be preserved, while a portion of the nutriment is to go into the sauce or gravy; less water is used than in making soup and it is cooked at a moderate heat for a long time. The pieces of meat best adapted for stewing are the pieces from the upper part of the shin, the aitch bone, the flank and the shoulder; it is better to use meat that has some fat and bone, as the stew will be richer.

You will be surprised to find under how many fanciful names the homely stew masquerades. We all know the plain Irish stew with its vegetables and dumplings cooked with the meat; I dare say many of you have often wondered, as I used to do when a little girl, while puzzling over the queer names in the cookery books, what a ragout might be. Well, it is nothing more or less than our friend, the stew, highly flavored with wine. A salmi is a stew of game, usually made from the left-over pieces of a game dinner; this is also quite highly flavored oftenest with currant jelly. A haricot is a stew with the meat and vegetables cut fine. Of course you all know that a chowder is a stew of fish, clams or oysters; and that a fricassee is a stew in which the meat is browned in fat, either before or after cooking in the hot water, and is served without vegetables. A pot-pie is a stew in which the dough is put on as a crust, covering the whole top of the kettle in which it is cooked instead of being used in balls as dumplings.

The vegetables that are principally used with stews are onions, potatoes, carrots and turnips; these should be cut small and added to the stew about half an hour before it is to be served. While the vegetables are boiling the kettle should be drawn toward the front of the stove, so that the water will more than simmer. If you have used the bones and fat in the preparation of the stew, you should remove them before adding the vegetables. (Dumplings will be taught in the next lesson, which will be on "batters.")

Now for one simple stew, one called in the Liverpool School, an "Exeter Stew." Use for every half pound of beef, half of an onion, one quarter each of turnip and carrot, two potatoes, salt and pepper to taste, a little flour, and water enough to cover. Wipe the meat, cut it into small pieces, removing any bits of crumbly bone that may adhere to it. Put the larger bones into a kettle and cover with cold water, melt the fat of the meat, brown the sliced onion in it and skim them out as soon as they are a fine yellow brown; dredge the bits of meat with flour, sprinkle them with salt and pepper and brown them in the onion-seasoned fat. Put them and the onions into the kettle in which the bone is boiling and add enough boiling water to cover. Simmer from two to three hours, or until the meat is tender; half an hour before serving add the other vegetables, which should have been cut in small dice; twenty minutes before serving add the potatoes, which have been washed and pared and cut into quarters, and parboiled five minutes. You should take out the fat and bone before adding the vegetables. When ready to serve, skim out the meat and potatoes upon a hot platter, thicken the gravy if you think it necessary, add seasoning, then pour it over the meat. Half a cup of stewed tomato, that has been strained, is an excellent addition. If you make this stew successfully you will no doubt eat it with as keen a relish as did the girls in School Kitchen No. 1 on the memorable day when they and I learned how to make an "Exeter Stew."

# CHAPTER VIII.

### A LESSON IN BATTERS.

BEATING EGGS.

IT usually happens that the first thing the young cook undertakes to do is to make cake. I think this will be found to be the experience of fully nine tenths of the women who have struggled up through experiment and endeavor until they have pretty well mastered the difficulties of the art. I couldn't tell you why it is so, but the fact remains undisputed and undisputable. I dare say, however, the reason is that every detail follows so quickly one upon another, that the result is very quickly attained. It usually happens, too, that after the cake is compounded, it is left by the maker in more experienced hands to be baked.

But in the school-kitchen the cake-making, or indeed the mixing of any batters, does not come until the pupils have mastered the stove, learned to make and keep a fire, and to cook simple food without mixing. Those of you who have carefully watched the lessons from the beginning will see that they came along in sequence, and that each step taken prepares the pupils for the next one. In this way the teaching is systematic and, as in other studies, a principle is not taken up until the one which goes before it is thoroughly understood. Now, at last, the girls in caps and aprons have come to a real mixing-lesson; a lesson in which flour is used for the first time. The teacher gives a little practical talk in chemistry, and shows them why the baking powder or the soda and cream of tartar, or the sour milk and soda are necessary in these compounds. I have no time, nor indeed is this the place to talk chemistry; all I can tell you is that the gas which is made by the acid and alkalies being mixed together is needed to make the batter light. I dare say most of you already know that. By her careful questioning the teacher sees that her pupils understand this bit of chemical teaching, a practical illustration of which they are to have in the lesson that is to follow the lecture and examination.

Batters are thin mixtures of liquid and flour, with the addition of the ingredients that are to make the gas. They are to be quickly prepared, and cooked at once, and, as a rule, are better eaten as soon as they are cooked, since they are likely to lose some of their lightness by standing. Batters also should be baked in a very quick oven. Indeed the lightness and delicacy of a batter-mixture, when cooked, depends upon the quickness with which it is prepared and baked.

You will learn, before you are through, that the term "batters" is a very elastic one, and covers all mixtures from griddle-cakes to muffins, taking in everything that comes between. People speak incorrectly of "frying" griddle-cakes Really they are baked on two sides on a heated surface. When anything is fried, it is dropped in hot fat, so that it is completely immersed. Doughnuts are fried, and pan-cakes, and some kinds of muffins; drop-cakes and griddle-cakes are baked on a hot griddle, one side being browned, then the cake turned and browned on the other side. Muffins, loaf-cake and gems, all of which come under the head of batter-mixtures, are baked in an oven.

Just a word here about frying, as possibly there may be no other place where it can so well be said. Of course you will understand that it is quite impossible to put within the limits of a series of chapters like this, the whole detail of a year's work. The best that could be done was to take the more prominent features, and give those, passing over other processes, or at the most merely hinting at them. The chief idea of this book is to show, as far as may be possibly done, the scope and thoroughness of the work, the systematic methods by which it is treated and the full arousal of a half-awakened interest all the country over, so that everywhere the school-kitchen will become as successful a feature of the school-system as it has grown to be in Boston. So about "frying": it is quite the habit of people to speak of frying, when they really mean something else. As in the griddle-cakes, when really the mixture is baked, so it is with other things. One often hears about frying fish or meat, when the process is *sautéing*, or browning one side at a time in a little fat. Frying is, as the teacher has told you, cooking by immersion, in very hot fat. I think you will understand the distinction in the terms, and will know when they are correctly used.

But to return to the lesson on batters. I had great fun, one day, in hearing this very lesson given as a practical lesson by one of the normal class to her classmates. These bright young women were "making-believe be little girls" with all their might; but such precocious little girls — how they did puzzle the teacher with their questions! One girl was set to build the fire. She had been taught just how to do it, but she had a theory of her own, evidently, that she had been longing for the opportunity to apply, and here it came. Well, she made her experiment and it was a disastrous failure; the fire refused to burn. It simply wouldn't; and the more she tried the more it refused, and all the dozen girls had the most mischievous twinkle in their eyes, and only waited for the lesson to be over to rally her in her theories. Which proved, my dear little amateur cooks who read this, that common sense is better than theory, and that there are some old-fashioned ways which we can't improve upon. The end of it was that the fire had to be made over from the very beginning, and at least half an hour of lesson-time was lost. It may be that it wasn't lost, after all; it has borne in upon this class of girls, that it won't do to try experiments in fire-building if one wants breakfast on time.

The simplest of all the batter-mixtures is the griddle-cake. This may be made with sweet milk and baking-powder, or with sour milk and soda. Some persons add an egg, but it really is not necessary; the cakes are just as light and toothsome without it as with it. Just here, as a preliminary to all batters, it will not be amiss to give the proportions of acids and alkalies in any mixture. If you are using soda and cream of tartar you will allow for every quart of flour, one teaspoonful of soda and two teaspoonfuls of cream of tartar. In measuring remember that the teaspoonfuls of soda must be level-full, while the cream of tartar should be rounded-full. The latter is always a fine, smooth powder, velvety to the touch, while the former is apt to grow lumpy. So it should be pulverized, then sifted before using, as you will then have more nearly correct proportions.

When you use sour milk you do not need the acid of the cream of tartar, but you want the soda to counteract the acidity in the milk, and the correct proportion is one level teaspoonful of soda to every pint of milk. In soft gingerbreads and some batter-puddings you will use molasses, and as this, in spite of its heavy clogging sweetness, contains acid you will need the soda to counteract it. If you are making a batter, the proportion of soda is one level teaspoonful to one cup of the molasses; if the dough is to be stiff — those will be considered later — one half a teaspoonful of soda is sufficient for the cup of molasses. If you use baking-powder, in place of cream of tartar and soda, the proportion will be one level teaspoonful of baking powder to each cup of flour or meal, whichever you use.

And now for the griddle-cakes. The rule on the school-kitchen cards, by which the class is cooking, gives the following proportions: one cup of flour; one saltspoonful of salt; one teaspoonful of baking powder; one scant cup of sweet milk, and one teaspoonful of melted butter. This may be varied by using sour milk in the same proportion as the sweet, and soda in place of baking powder. If any one is so fortunate as to live on a dairy farm, buttermilk may be substituted for the sour milk, in which case the tablespoonful of melted butter may be omitted. Sift the dry ingredients together, that is, the flour, baking powder (or soda) and salt; then add the milk, making a batter about like thick cream. Add the melted butter last. Cook on a well-greased griddle that is hot enough to bake the cakes without burning them. When the upper side has filled with bubbles turn the cake over and brown the other side.

There are some persons who object to the

use either of baking powder or soda and cream of tartar, but who make batters light without them by excessive beating. Among the quick cakes prepared by them in this way are "popovers;" these are as light as vanity and there is just about as much to them. If you wish to try them you may use one cup of flour, one cup of milk, an egg, and one salt-spoonful of salt. Sift the salt and flour together and add half of the quantity of milk slowly, making a smooth paste; when it is well mixed and no lumps of flour, no matter how tiny, are left, add the remainder of the milk and the egg, which has been beaten to perfect lightness. Beat the whole together thoroughly, and cook at once in hot buttered gem pans or earthen cups, for half an hour or until the cakes are well "popped over," inventing their name, and of a delicious golden brown. You may use these as breakfast cakes, eaten with butter like muffins, or you may serve them for dessert with a rich, hot sauce. You will like them either way.

When the "big blizzard" struck New York, a lady well-known as an editor and writer, got snow-bound in a little town just outside the city; so prisoned were the residents by the elements, that neither "butcher nor baker, nor candlestick-maker" could get at them, and as there were quite a number of persons in the house at which this lady was staying, the provisions soon grew scanty. Among the necessary articles which gave out were eggs; and there were none to put in the muffins for breakfast, when suddenly some body remembered "snow pan-cakes," and they were speedily concocted, and so successful were they that every body went away, when the blockade was raised, singing their praises. The story got into all the papers, and so did the receipt; but the cooking schools were ahead of the papers, for they had already taught the girls how to make them. Use one half cup of flour, and one saltspoonful of salt (sifted together), add one half a cup of milk and beat very thoroughly; when it is beaten stir lightly in a heaping tablespoonful of newly-fallen snow. Cook like large griddle-cakes, and while hot spread with butter, sugar and nutmeg, or with jam, roll them over and over like a jelly roll, and eat them at once; don't talk until the last mouthful is finished, then be as ecstatic as you please.

And now I am going to tell you, just as Miss Hope did the girls in School-Kitchen No. 1, how to make an old-fashioned molasses gingerbread. The following are the proportions: one half cup of molasses, one half tablespoonful of ginger, one saltspoonful of salt, one half teaspoonful of soda, one tablespoonful of clear beef dripping — or you may use butter — one quarter of a cup of hot water (boiling) and one cup of flour. The ginger, soda and salt are added to the molasses; the softened dripping is then put in, and the mixture beaten well together; next the boiling water is added, then the flour; beat again thoroughly, pour into a well-greased shallow pan and bake in a hot oven. It will take about twenty minutes to bake the loaf.

And now for the dumplings which I promised you when we had the stew. To a pint of flour, use half a teaspoonful of salt, two teaspoonfuls of baking-powder and one scant cup of milk. Sift together the flour, baking-powder and salt. Stir in the milk to make a soft dough. Drop them, with the spoon, into the boiling stew. They will rest on the meat and potato; cover them, and let them cook ten minutes. Do not lift the cover in that time. Serve as soon as done. You will find them very nice and light.

I will give you the School corn-cake, and that must finish the batters, although there is more that might be said.

Don't you wish the School-Kitchen was an accomplished fact in your town? And are you all working toward that end? You know you have something to do about making public opinion in all the matters in which you are deeply interested. Fathers and mothers are pretty sure to feel what their children feel, and to desire to give them that they want, when they feel that the " want " is sensible and right. And who is the " public " that is so much talked about if it isn't the aggregate of fathers and mothers all through the community?

But we'll never get to the corn-cake if we don't go on. We'll make ready with one cup of flour, one half cup of fine yellow cornmeal, one quarter of a cup of sugar, one half teaspoonful of salt, one tablespoonful of cream of tartar — if you use sweet milk, omit it if the milk is sour — one half teaspoonful of soda, one cup of milk — either sweet or sour — one egg, one tablespoonful of dripping or butter. Mix all the dry things together; beat the egg, add the milk to it, put it into the mixed dry ingredients, mix well together, and last of all add the melted butter. Beat well and bake in muffin rings or a shallow pan for about twenty minutes. Then you have a corn-cake that is good enough for your breakfast, or mine, or Queen Victoria's.

# CHAPTER IX.

### BREAD—MAKING.

KNEADING.

AS I sit writing there floats in from the pantry beyond the kitchen a sweet girlish voice singing the dear old hymn,

"O mother dear, Jerusalem,"

and as a sort of accompaniment comes a soft thumping sound. This peculiar sort of accompaniment I have learned to know is made by the slipping of the bread-board on the table, as the fourteen-year-old daughter kneads the dough that she is just setting for to-morrow morning's baking.

She took the task of making the family bread during one of the domestic emergencies that occur in every family, and she has kept it for three months, until she is an accomplished bread-maker, and enjoys her work, not minding it at all, nor considering it a hard task. She does not go to the Public School Cooking Classes because she does not live in Boston; but she has learned to do a good many things, and likes trying experiments. It is odd, isn't it, that I should write this chapter on bread to the accompaniment of the kneading and the little glad song of the maker?

But you and I must run away from the Dedham kitchen and its happy occupant, and find ourselves one of the class in the School-Kitchen. It is an important day in the school when bread is to be made. The girls really believe then that they are genuine cooks. They put on their aprons and caps with greater alacrity than usual, full of the importance of the occasion and anxious to begin.

Of course the rules for yeast and for bread that I am going to give you are the ones in use at the school, and as I have seen and tasted the bread made there, I think them very good. The yeast really used is the compressed yeast that is so universally liked by housekeepers, but as there are liable to be occasions when this yeast is not obtainable, it has been considered wise to teach the pupils to make their own yeast. Of course this is not at all likely to occur in towns where shops are convenient and one can run out and fill one's household needs at an instant's notice. But if one lives at a distance from stores, it is quite a convenience to have one's own yeast jug to go to whenever bread is to be made. Most housekeepers living on farms and far away from shopping centers keep their own yeast constantly on hand, never allowing themselves to be quite out of it, generally using the last cupful to start the new supply with.

It is not a difficult matter to make the yeast, as you shall see. But first I must tell you that there is a good deal of practical chemistry in this lesson, which you and I must omit as we have not the space for more than the practical working facts. Indeed, there is a scientific reason for everything that is done in practical cooking, some of which I dare say you may have found out for yourself. If you haven't you must manage somehow to get the school-training, and then you will know all about it.

And now for the yeast, made by using the following ingredients in these proportions:

One large potato, one tablespoonful of hops loose, one pint of boiling water, one heaping tablespoonful of flour, one heaping teaspoonful of sugar, one heaping teaspoonful of salt, one quarter of a teaspoonful of ginger, one half a yeast cake dissolved in half a cup of lukewarm water, or one half a cup of yeast. Wash the potato well, pare it and put it in cold water to soak. Steep the hops in the boiling water.

Mix the flour, sugar, ginger and salt in a large bowl, then grate the potato into this flour mixture; let the hop-water boil for one minute, then strain it over the potato and flour, and mix it as quickly as possible. If it does not thicken like starch place it over the fire for a few minutes. If it is too thick add boiling water until it is as thick as cream; set it aside to cool, and when it is lukewarm add the yeast. Set in a warm place to rise, until it is frothy and light. Beat it down every half-hour. When it is risen sufficiently put it in a jar or a glass bottle, and keep it cool. When you have to take some of the yeast out do not take the jar into a warm place, but pour it out where it is kept, and mind that the cork is replaced at once.

You will see that the potato is not cooked, but is grated raw. Now many of the rules that are in use in families call for boiled potatoes. I do not suppose that the yeast itself is any better made with the uncooked potatoes, *but it keeps better*. It will sour quicker when the cooked potato is used, just as any cooked vegetables spoil more quickly than the uncooked ones. Perhaps some of you may be able to give your mothers a point just here in regard to yeast-making. It is more trying both to fingers and temper to grate the raw potato than to mash the cooked one, but the result will be better, and that is worth taking a little extra trouble for, isn't it? In fact, my little cooks, you will find as you go along that the trouble taken does repay you, no matter what it is that you are doing. And in nothing does one get so satisfactorily rewarded for the extra care as in cooking. Ask your mother if it isn't so, you little doubter; and you too, who think "it's all nonsense to take such pains; it won't be any better for it." All this will be borne in upon you in the School Kitchen, and you will soon become assured that there is no royal road to anything that is worth doing, and that learning to cook is very much like all the rest.

But now comes the bread-making, the yeast

having been made and bottled. (In regard to the respective merits of the yeasts; in general results they are the same, but it must be acknowledged that the compressed yeast makes the bread finer and whiter than the home-made yeast does, but it is no sweeter, nor has it a better flavor.) The rule here given will make either one loaf of bread or a pan of biscuits. You increase the rule as you desire a larger quantity. Use one cup of milk or water, lukewarm, one half a teaspoonful of salt, one half a teaspoonful of sugar, one quarter of a cup of yeast, or one quarter of a yeast cake dissolved in one quarter of a cup of water, and from three to three and a half cups of flour. If you use milk you must heat it to boiling in the double heater; mere scalding will not do; it must be boiled; the bread will keep better, and the dough will not turn sour in rising, as it often will do in warm weather, even when great care is exercised. But the School Kitchen girls are taught to raise their bread dough with water,

Sift the flour into the mixing bowl, which should be of earthen ware, as this holds the heat better than tin, and makes the bread rise more quickly. Mix the salt, sugar and yeast, then add the milk or water, and pour into the bowl which holds the flour; mix it thoroughly with a knife, and then, when it is well mixed, and is stiff enough to knead, turn it out on to a well-floured board, and knead it until it is soft and elastic and can be worked without any flour. You need not make hard work of the kneading; it is lightness and quickness of touch rather than an expenditure of strength which is required. What is wanted is to get it well-mixed, so that every particle shall be permeated with the yeast, and the whole mass shall be perfectly smooth and free from lumps.

I once had a cook who was trying to teach the second girl to make bread. She said to me one day, after we had been treated to some bread of the pupil's making that was far below the standard: " Indeed, ma'am, and it's no use trying to teach Nellie to make bread, she cannot do it; she is too heavy-handed; she'll never make a cook."

I didn't quite see what Maggie meant, but I found out by watching. The girl moved clumsily; she touched things as though her hand was of iron; she clutched rather than held; there was no lightness, nor alertness to any of her movements. She was hopelessly "heavy," and her hands spoiled the bread rather than lightened it. I have seen a few people like her since, and I have found out in every case that they were not good cooks. No matter how hard they tried, they could not succeed. It was in the hopeless heaviness of their movements. Now all this won't be taught you in the cooking school, because there it is the duty of the teacher to make the pupils do things, and never let them think they cannot. But I give you this information out of my own experience; it will perhaps assist you in time to come when it shall fall to your lot to look for the new servant girl.

The bread has been "put to rise" in the bowl, neatly covered with a clean bread cloth, with a pan closely put over it to keep out the air, so that a crust may not form on the outside, but that the whole mass may be kept soft. The lesson is over. We are to come again for the baking.

We left our bread in a warm, sheltered place, where it should be subject to no sudden change of temperature, and we have come again to find it beautifully risen, ready to make into loaf or biscuit. When well-risen it should be double its original bulk; work it over in the bowl, doubling it from the edges toward the center until it is smooth, let it rise again, which it will do quickly, until it is double its bulk, then shape into loaves and set to rise closely covered, in the pans in which it is to be baked. Let it rise until it is light, then bake in a hot oven, or one so hot that you can hold the hand in twelve seconds without getting too hot. It you have a cooking thermometer, which, by the way, very few do have, it should register four hundred degrees. At first you will have to take counsel with some one to whom bread-baking is not a novelty.

Have any of you ever had anything to do with those exasperating people, who, when asked for any instruction, always say "use your own judgment"? Aren't they provoking? Why, how is the novice in anything to have any judgment to use? What is "judgment" but the outcome of experience? Knowledge of any kind doesn't come by intuition; it is the result of repeated experiment. Now the next time any one tells you to "use your judgment" when you ask them how long to bake the loaf, or how hot to have the oven, or how much baking-powder to put into the muffins — get them to define judgment for you, and then ask them very respectfully how you have had time or opportunity to acquire it.

In the meantime bake your bread from forty to sixty minutes; see that it properly browns, a lovely golden color, and that it has a hollow sound when you thump it with your knuckle.

## CHAPTER X.

### FISH AND EGG DISHES.

IT is a part of the economical plan of the School-Kitchen system, that the special lessons on fish and eggs should be given at the time of the year when they are the most plentiful, and the least expensive. Nature has a wise way of arranging things, and it is quite in accordance with her usual wisdom and forethought that both these articles of food should be the least costly at the season when the system most demands them; that is, in the spring and summer. In the cold weather of winter we need the heat-giving of meat; but in the summer, and indeed in the spring, when the first warm days are coming on, the meat in any quantity is distasteful, and one likes best the fresh eggs and the delicate fish. You will probably understand, through your lessons in chemistry and in physiology, that meat stimulates nerves and brain, and that this stimulation should be avoided in warm weather.

Fish and eggs are given in separate lessons, but we take them together to save space. To begin with the fish. There really is no more valuable food in all the list. It is easy of digestion, it is inexpensive, and it is plenty. It has not the amount of nutrition which meat possesses, but it has sufficient, and as it has a large amount of phosphorus, it is very beneficial. Fish should be eaten perfectly fresh, while the flesh is yet firm; otherwise all its beneficent qualities are lost, and it becomes poisonous. Never buy fish when the flesh is soft and flabby, unless you desire a genuine fit of indigestion, if not a severe and painful illness.

In one of the school-kitchens a class of boys has been admitted during the winter just past, and it has proven a very bright class.

"We had a prime fish-chowder to day," said one of these boys to his teacher, on coming to the school in the afternoon.

"Did you make it?" queried the teacher.

"No. I gave my mother a cooking-school lesson, and saw that she did it just right. Father says it was the best he ever tasted."

And now I am going to give you the school-kitchen rule for that "prime fish-chowder." You will observe the following proportions in preparing your ingredients:

To every pound of fish — cod or haddock is the best — use a one-inch cube of salt pork, half of an onion, two potatoes, a speck of pepper, one tablespoonful of flour, one tablespoonful of butter, one cup of milk and two crackers.

See that the fish is carefully cleaned and cut into pieces after the bone is removed. You may bone the fish yourself, or the marketman will do it for you. Cook the bones of the fish and the head for half an hour in boiling water, then strain the water from it and save. Cut the salt pork and onion into dice, and fry until they are a light brown. In the meantime slice the potatoes, and let them scald for five minutes, pour off the water and add to the scalded potatoes the bone water and the pork fat, which has been strained to remove the pieces of onion and the solid bits of pork. Put this over the fire in a stew-pan, and when it is boiling add the fish, and simmer ten minutes or until the potatoes are tender; last of all add the pepper, butter, milk and crackers.

I am sure if any of you try this receipt you will find that it is delicious, even if you do not, like myself, care much about the ordinary fish-chowder. You see this is an extraordinary one.

There are a variety of ways of cooking fish, but they are most generally baked or broiled; sometimes they are boiled, and sometimes fried; but the most wholesome ways are the two first mentioned.

The fish which are the oftenest used for baking are cod, haddock, blue-fish, bass, shad and small salmon. The fish should be well cleaned — indeed that is necessary whatever way it is to be cooked — wiped dry and rubbed with salt. It should then be stuffed and the edges sewed together. The stuffing will be prepared by the following rule, and it is sufficient for a fish weighing from four to six pounds. Use one cup of cracker-crumbs, one salt-spoonful of salt, one salt-spoonful of pepper, and one tablespoonful of chopped onion, one teaspoonful of chopped parsley, one teaspoonful of capers, one teaspoonful of chopped pickles, and a quarter of a cup of melted butter. The crackers should be moistened with hot water if you desire a moist stuffing, otherwise it will be dry and crumbly. After the fish is stuffed cut gashes two inches apart on each side. Put narrow strips of fat salt pork in the gashes, and in the pan under the fish. Place the fish upright in the pan by skewering the head one way and the tail another. Dredge the fish with flour. Put it into a hot oven without water; when the flour is brown, baste with the pork fat, and baste often. It is done when the flesh separates easily from the bone. Remove it carefully to a hot platter, draw out the strings or skewers and serve with drawn butter or egg sauce.

You "don't know how to make either?" Well, you will very soon, if you will only follow the directions that the cooking-school teacher will give you. Here is the drawn butter:

Use one pint of hot water or milk — the latter is by far the best, if you can get it — one scant cup of butter, two tablespoonfuls of flour, one half a teaspoonful of salt, and one half a salt-spoonful of pepper. Put half the butter into a sauce-pan over the fire; let it melt, but not burn; when it is melted add the dry flour and mix well. Add the hot water or milk, a little at a time, and stir rapidly as it thickens. When perfectly smooth add the remainder of the butter by degrees, and stir until it is dissolved. Add the salt and pepper. When carefully made this sauce should be free from lumps; but if not smooth, strain it before serving. Now egg sauce is simply this drawn butter with two or three hard boiled eggs, chopped or sliced, added to it.

The fish that are broiled are mackerel, white-fish, blue-fish that are too small to bake, trout, small cod, shad, or any other thin fish; also slices of halibut, salmon, and other thick fish. When the entire fish is broiled it should be split down the back, and the head and tail removed. It is a good plan to remove the backbone also. If the fish is oily it needs only to be sprinkled with salt and pepper; if it is dry, the fish should be spread with half-melted butter before broiling.

The double wire broiler should be well-greased; put the thickest edge of the fish next the middle of the broiler; broil the flesh side first until it is brown, lifting it up often that it may not burn. The other side should be broiled just enough to crisp the skin. Of course the time the fish should cook will vary with its thickness. When it is done the flesh will look white and firm, and will separate easily from the bone. After the fish is cooked, season it with butter, salt, and pepper, and lemon juice. The latter may be omitted if preferred.

Now the lesson about eggs.

It is surprising how many people there are who do not use eggs as a matter of course for an article of diet. In the spring time, particularly, they are more healthful than heavy matter, and they are then at their cheapest, so it is not extravagant to use them freely. Many persons who do not care specially for them when boiled, or who have grown tired of them from constantly having them cooked in that way, would like them if they were made into an omelet or dropped on toast; they somehow seem more delicate when cooked in either of these ways, and they look very much nicer coming to the table. It is not the easiest thing in the world to make an omelet; indeed it is a little troublesome until one gets quite accustomed to it. But practise will soon enable one to not only prepare, but to cook — which is the difficult part — an omelet which shall rival that of the experienced cook. For a small omelet you will use two eggs, two tablespoonfuls of milk, one salt-spoonful of salt, one salt-spoonful of pepper. Beat the yolks of the eggs until they are light and creamy, and to these beaten yolks add the milk, salt and pepper. Beat the whites until they are stiff and dry. Stir them lightly into the yolks until they are just covered, but do not beat them. When your smooth omelet pan or small spider is hot, rub it round the edge with a teaspoonful of butter; let the butter run over the pan, so that it is entirely covered, and when it is bubbling turn in the omelet quickly. Cook very carefully, not over the hottest part of the fire, else it would burn, until it is slightly browned underneath; put it in the oven so that the top may dry, but do not let it burn; fold toward the right, put a hot platter over the pan, then turn all over, so that the omelet will drop evenly on to the platter.

This is really the most difficult of all the egg dishes, and the only one that it is necessary to give, since all the others are so simple and in such constant use that it would be like relating an old story to tell about them.

It may seem to you that this chapter is largely filled with "rules." Possibly; but there is so little to say in a general way about either of the food articles, that the space may be given to detailed work. Everything which has been described is so simple that it may be tried at home, and with little fear of failure.

In connection with the egg-lesson simple cake batters are taught, and these lessons the girls seem to enjoy very much. Somehow girls almost all like cake-making. That, and making delicate desserts, are the fancy work of cooking. It is all very well, too, in its way, and a certain amount of it, but after all it is the every-day substantial food that is the most necessary, and that must be done.

# CHAPTER XI.

### INVALID COOKERY.

THERE is no more important branch of cookery than that which is devoted to the sick room, and it shows wisdom on the part of those in charge at the schools that they have so emphasized this portion of the work, and laid out the lessons pertaining to it so carefully.

Probably most of you know, from experience, how very greatly trifles are magnified when one is ill. Matters that are not of the slightest consequence in health, become very important when one is held down by sickness. Things that would be passed over usually, will then worry and fret one indescribably; while the least act that is kindly and thoughtful will be magnified in the same proportion.

One of the first things I remember in my life, is being very ill with the measles. I could not have been more than three or four years old. I had a nightdress, which in addition to the ruffles that ornamented it, had a double row of stitching on the bands of neck and sleeves. I was particularly fond of that stitching, and I used to watch for the day when it would be the time to wear that nightdress. I really grieved when I had to take it off to have it washed. One morning I had been bathed, and I was waiting

CARING FOR THE SICK.

for the clean nightdress; there wasn't much anticipation about it, for I had worn the stitched one the day before. I was lying listlessly, until the fresh robe should be brought. As it came my childish eyes caught the sight of stitching. I cried for very joy, I was so happy. The dear mother, who always did the sweetest and nicest things for her little girl, had sat up after the nervous, troublesome child was asleep, and had with her own kind fingers stitched the little robe. After that she stitched them all, and I know I got well much quicker for it. Now I dare say this seems a silly little story to tell, but it proves what I said — that trifles affect sick people much more than they do those who are well.

A friend was telling me, not long since, about an experience she had while ill. "I was so ashamed of myself," she said, "but I could not help it. My nurse had gone out, and I took the fancy that I wanted some cream toast. I asked my daughter, a girl of about fifteen, to make it for me. She did so, and when she brought it to me I cried just as hard as I could cry. She had put it on to a plate that I particularly hated, and the very sight of it took away my appetite. The child was as distressed as I was, for she really wanted to serve me. I could have boxed my own ears when I got better and thought it over, but it was a very serious matter at the time. However, it was a lesson my girl will never forget, and I am sure the next time she is called upon to serve an invalid, she will bring the best china plate in the house."

Now part of the teaching at the school is how to serve as well as how to cook. The tray for the invalid must be carefully prepared; the tray cloth must be spotless, and the dishes nice and fresh. Then, do not put on so much food that it takes away the appetite to look at it; it is easy to replenish if more is wanted. What you are to do is to coax the unwilling appetite, by literally making things look "good enough to eat." Take care that nothing spills in carrying, from cup, bowl or glass. If hot food is to be served, cover it so that it may not be cooled while it is taken from the kitchen to the sick room. A little heed will enable you to do all this, and you may be as adept at serving your invalid as you are in cooking for her.

Probably nothing — unless it be gruel — is oftener used in the invalid's room than toast. It seems a very simple thing to make and yet nothing can be more easily spoiled. It may be burned, when the scorched taste will make it unpalatable ; or it may be so quickly done that the outside will be hard, while the inside of the slice will be clammy and consequently indigestible. It should be neither; but should be dry all through, and of a delicate golden brown. Stale bread should be used, and it should be cut in even slices, about a quarter of an inch thick ; no thicker, certainly. When it is cut put it on a toaster or fork, and move it gently over the fire until it is dry ; then hold it nearer the fire until it is a beautiful golden brown. If plain toast is wanted serve it at once, hot and dry. If plain water toast, or as it is oftener called, "wet butter toast," is desired, you will prepare the slices as for the dry toast; have a shallow pan with one pint of boiling water and one half a teaspoonful of salt in it. Dip each slice of dry toast quickly in the water, then spread with butter and serve very hot. Perhaps it will be milk toast your invalid will want; then you will observe the following rules: Prepare the bread, as if for the plain dry toast. For the "dip" you will use materials in the following proportion:

One cup of milk, scalded, one half a tablespoonful of corn starch, or one tablespoonful of flour; one half a tablespoonful of butter, and one half a teaspoonful of salt. Melt the butter in a granite saucepan, add the dry corn starch or flour, mix well together, taking care that the mixture does not burn; add one third of the milk, which has been heated in the double boiler, stir well as it boils and thickens, then add half the remaining milk, stir again, until it is smooth and entirely free from lumps; when it is quite smooth add the remainder of the milk and the salt. Pour this dip between each slice of toast, and over the whole. If you want the slices to be soft, dip them in hot salted water before pouring the dip or sauce over them.

You will follow these same directions in making toast for the family table. They are at once the easiest and the most correct. You will find them prove very nice, too, I am sure.

Perhaps this is as good a place as any to tell you that the cream for the toast is the "white sauce" or "cream sauce" that is used for so many purposes in cooking. Whenever you have a rule given you that says "make a white sauce," you may turn to this cream dip, and there you have it. Made a bit thicker it is used to mix croquettes, to cream fish, to pour over vegetables that you serve *à la crême*, as it is called. Like many another high-sounding article of food, it is very simple when reduced to its lowest terms. This sauce with egg boiled hard and cut up in it is "egg sauce;" with capers added to it, it is "caper sauce;" you may flavor it in as many ways as you desire, with lemon, onion juice, cayenne, the kind of seasoning you use depending upon the use you are to make of it. As you progress in your knowledge of cooking you will soon come to know that many an every-day dish is hidden under a fine, high-sounding name.

Of course it is quite necessary that you shall know how to make gruels, for they are much used in sickness. One of the most commonly-used gruels is that made from oatmeal. The girls at the school kitchen get to the point where they do this very nicely, and I think one of the most satisfactory features of the cooking exhibition that was given one spring in connection with the sewing exhibition, was the "invalid cookery." There were glasses of beef tea and lemonade, molds of blanc-mange and bowls of gruel. More comment was elicited by these dishes than by any of the others. For some reason or other the visitors seemed surprised at seeing them; they evidently had not understood the full scope of the School Kitchen work.

But we must make the gruel, and not content ourselves with merely talking of it. Pound one half a cup of coarse oatmeal until it is mealy; the best way to do this is to tie it in a coarse cloth, and pound it with a wooden mallet. It is thus bruised without waste. Put it into a tumbler with cold water; stir it well and when the sediment has settled pour off the mealy water into a saucepan. Fill it again with water, stirring it, letting it settle and pouring off as before. Do this a third time, being very careful each time not to disturb the sediment in pouring. Boil this water which you turned off for twenty minutes, stirring it often. Add one saltspoonful of salt, and if it is too thick add a little cream or milk.

In making the gruel this way you get all the nourishing quality of the meal, as that mixes with the water, and only the hulls, or coarse indigestible portion is left. It is not a difficult piece of work, and I think you will find it very satisfactory.

The old-fashioned "milk porridge" is another of the invalid dishes that is taught. It is rarely one finds anybody except the trained nurse or the old-time housekeeper who makes it nowadays. I don't think it is so palatable as either the oatmeal or Indian meal gruel; but there are some diseases in which it is better for the patient than either of these. The doctor will always order it when he finds it needed, and all you have to do is to follow the school rule for making, and your invalid will get just what the doctor meant she should have. You will use two dozen raisins quartered, two cups of milk, one tablespoonful of flour and one saltspoonful of salt. Boil the raisins in a little water for twenty minutes; let the water boil away and add the milk; when this boils add the flour, which you have rubbed to a thin paste with cold water, and boil it for at least eight or ten minutes. Season it with salt, and strain before you serve it. You see how very simple all this is. Surely your sick-room cookery is not going to prove very difficult.

The delicate appetite of the convalescent will be tempted almost invariably by blanc-mange. There are many preparations from which it may be made — farina, corn starch or arrowroot; but that which is the most highly considered is made from the Irish moss; the genuine blanc-mange, as it was originally made. You will take to a quarter of a cup of Irish moss one pint of milk, one half a saltspoonful of salt, and one half a teaspoonful of vanilla. Soak the moss in cold water until it is soft; pick it over carefully and wash it, removing anything that may adhere to it, so that it shall be perfectly clean. When it is thus prepared tie it in a thin lace bag, and put it into the double boiler with the milk; boil until you find that it will thicken when it is dropped upon a cold plate. That is your test for it. Then add the salt, strain it and add the flavoring. Wet a mold or a cup in cold water, and pour the blanc-mange into it; when it cools put it upon the ice until you wish to serve it; when you are ready for it turn it out into a pretty dish, and serve sugar and cream with it. Like the toast, the blanc-mange may be made in this way for tea, or for a dinner dessert. It is "none too good" for any of us, I assure you.

Irish moss also is used to make a jelly that is at once palatable and delicate, and is very grateful to the fever-parched lips of a sick person. Use one half a cup of Irish moss, four figs, one pint of boiling water, one lemon or orange, one third of a cup of sugar. Prepare the moss as for the blanc-mange by soaking, picking over and washing. Put it into the boiling water, add the figs and the thin rind of the lemon. Simmer until the moss is dissolved, then add the lemon or orange juice and the sugar, and strain into a cold wet mold.

Beef tea is an important adjunct in the list of invalid dishes. It is used to stimulate and nourish when the system has need of quick recuperation. This tea that is given here is the genuine extract of beef, containing all the strengthening properties, and the full nourishment of the meat. It is not always given in its full strength, but diluted with hot water until it is at the strength desired by the physician. In making it always select the juciest beef, quite without regard to tenderness. Indeed, the tenderer the meat is, the less juicy it will be found. The lower part of the round is usually found to be the best for beef tea. It must be absolutely free from fat, only the lean meat being available. Cut the beef into quarter-inch dice-shaped pieces, and put them in a wide-mouthed bottle; cover the bottle and set it on a tin in a kettle of cold water. Set this over the fire and heat it gradually. When it comes to a boil keep it gently simmering until the meat is perfectly white, looking like pieces of India rubber. Then strain out the juice, press it all out from the pieces of meat, and season to the taste with salt. In making your tea this way you see that you will get the actual juice of the beef; every particle is extracted, so that the nourishing properties are all obtained.

You should know how to make at least one or two cooling drinks for the sick room. Suppose we take lemonade and eggnog. For the first use to every lemon one tablespoonful of sugar, and one cup of boiling water. Remove the peel in very thin parings, put them into a bowl, add the boiling water, and let it stand ten minutes, covered. Add the lemon juice and the sugar, stir it well to dissolve the sugar. If hot lemonade is desired, strain it at once and it is ready; if you wish it cold, set it aside and when it is cool, strain it. You may add ice if you desire, and the doctor allows it. To make an eggnog, you will separate the white and yolk of one egg, and beat the yolk with a tablespoonful of sugar until it is light and creamy; add to this one half a cup of milk; then beat the white of the egg to a foam, and stir it lightly into the beaten yolk, sugar and milk. It is a delicious and a nourishing drink. Try it some day, when hungry and tired, and see if I'm not right.

## CHAPTER XII.

NORMAL TRAINING.

IT has been quite impossible, within the limits of these chapters, to give the entire work of the school-kitchens for a year, but if I have been successful in even indicating what is done in the line of accomplishment I shall be glad. I hope you don't find figures stupid, because I wish to give you a few facts to remember, and use; for you know you are to be earnest workers in the endeavor to have school-kitchens introduced into every city and town in the country. Do you think this a very hard task? Well, if any one of you had the entire work to accomplish, you might hesitate before beginning it. But there are a great many of you to undertake the labor. Recall what I· said not long since about forming public opinion. It would be impossible for any one of you to work for the establishment of school-kitchens all over the United States, but each one may use her influence in whatever place she chances to be, and it will be the united effort of so many that will tell in the result.

Of course it is quite necessary that you shall be in possession of facts so that you may present them to the people whom you wish to convince. It does no good merely to make a general statement — skeptical people have a way of demanding proof of your assertion — and I hope to give you something that shall serve you well in your work as an advocate of industrial training.

When the school-kitchens were first established in Boston, some of the people who had opposed them most earnestly said they would interfere with the regular school-duties; and that if so much time was given to outside work the scholarship would suffer. But it has not;

on the contrary, teachers say that the girls come back to their studies refreshed from the change of occupation. You will probably meet this same argument — it is a favorite one — and there is your reply ready.

After the school had been in operation about a year, all the mothers who had daughters attending the kitchens, were asked to give their opinion of the school and its results. Out of over eight hundred mothers who were seen, only two expressed themselves as opposed or indifferent. All the rest were pleased, and grateful for the opportunity given to their daughters.

Many of them said that they had not been able to give their girls instruction at home for lack of time, others could not risk the waste of materials, and they were glad to have them have the training because it was what every girl needed; every one testified to the good the teaching had accomplished and told with pardonable pride what the girls had done at home. Some of them had even taught their mothers better ways of doing things than they had ever known, and you would have been both pleased and amused to hear the proud tone in the mother's voice, as she told of her little girl's achievement. One poor Russian Jewess who could with difficulty express herself in English, said to the visitor:

"I wish much thank to the congregation for give my girl to make so much of good."

She did well with her limited English, I think.

And now about the cost, which is an important consideration. The greatest expense comes in the fitting up of the kitchen. I can really give you no idea what that will be, even approximately, but I am sure if you were to ask Miss Homans, No. 26 Berwick Park, Boston, she would give you all the information you would need, and help you in any way in which she could, for no one is more interested in this work than she.

Then there would be the salary of the teacher; that would be the same as is paid to any grammar-school teacher. Sometimes two or three small towns that are near together employ the same teacher, each town paying a proportionate part of the salary, and in this way doing what they might not feel able to do if each one had to bear the whole expense. Here you see one of the practical workings of co-operation, concerning which so much is said nowadays. I can tell you this much about the cost of material, however: the cost for each pupil for a lesson is a fraction less than two cents. No one can complain much about that, and be reasonable. If you are asked if it is possible to keep the expense as small in other places as in Boston, you can assure your questioner that it is.

The Boston normal training-school for cooking-teachers provides that the teaching shall be uniform, and the course studied is to be adopted in every school, and this insures a uniform cost.

This school has already graduated several pupils, and every one has found a place waiting for her when she has graduated. You can see by this that the work is being carried forward as rapidly as teachers can be got ready. The great danger is in beginning the work before you are altogether prepared. There is as much danger in undue haste, as there is in delay. I am not altogether certain that there isn't more. In any important matter like this it is safe to make haste slowly. No matter how anxious you are to see this work begin in your own town, wait until you can secure a teacher trained in the normal school, and do not fall into the mistaken notion that anybody can teach cooking who can cook. A mistake at the beginning would be fatal, and you could never again awaken interest in the subject.

Some of you may be specially interested in this training-school and for such I will say a little more about what is done there. In the first place, every applicant for admission must be acquainted with the theory of teaching, and it is considered a great point in her favor if she is a graduate of some Normal school. She should possess that particular qualification for the work — a liking for it; and she should determine to devote herself to it to the exclusion of all other branches, and be a power in her line of teaching.

There is no use in taking up any work in a half-hearted way; and if a pupil does not show herself disposed to do her best in the school, her continuance in the class is not encouraged. The teachers very soon discover if a student is lacking in the ability to do the work, and if there is any doubt of her ultimate success as a teacher of cookery she is kindly advised to turn her efforts in another direction. That is fair treatment, certainly, and kindly too. For the whole future of a girl may be spoiled by allowing her to make a failure when good advice, honestly given, might have turned her in the direction of success. And that is why

I am so glad of the interest and care that the managers of this particular school give to the pupils.

When a student has taken the course, passed the examination, and received her certificate, then she may feel that she is well equipped for the work, for no certificate would be given her had she not won it, you may be sure. The course of study includes, beside cooking, lessons in chemistry by the most competent teachers, and with the practice lessons in both branches, there are frequent lectures by well-know specialists.

And now for the results with the pupils of the public schools. I have been often asked whether any real good was accomplished by the training — that is, whether the children did any of the work at home which they were taught at the school. I may best reply to this question by quoting from the report made by the committee on manual training. During one year the Boston Public School girls cooked over seventeen thousand dishes at home. There were two thousand under instruction, so you may easily reckon how much each girl did. Of course some always do more than others, that is so in everything, you know. But the pupils of the schools are required to tell the teacher what they do at home, and how successful the work is, because only in that way is it possible to get at the results of the general work.

If you could see into some of the homes, and know what of comfort has come to them since the girls have learned how to cook well, you would be soon convinced that there is a moral as well as a practical side to the matter. At least one man has been led to give up his practice of going daily to the saloon at eleven o'clock for the drink of whiskey to "set him up," by the nice cup of chocolate and the corncake which his little daughter gives him for breakfast in place of the sloppy tea and dry baker's bread which he used to have. It is much easier to be good when one is comfortably fed than when one is put off with insufficient and illy-cooked food. So you see you have a moral as well as a statistical argument.

And now, dear girls, whom I have come to love very dearly, even without a glimpse of your faces, good-by, and, as Tiny Tim says,

"God bless us, every one!"

www.ingramcontent.com/pod-product-compliance
Lightning Source LLC
Chambersburg PA
CBHW031448160426
43195CB00010BB/904